JONATHAN SWIFT

Modern Critical Views

These and other titles in preparation

Modern Critical Views

JONATHAN SWIFT

Edited and with an introduction by
Harold Bloom
Sterling Professor of the Humanities
Yale University

CHELSEA HOUSE PUBLISHERS ◇ 1986
New York ◇ New Haven ◇ Philadelphia

© 1986 by Chelsea House Publishers, a division of Chelsea House
Educational Communications, Inc.
    133 Christopher Street, New York, NY 10014
    345 Whitney Avenue, New Haven, CT 06511
    5041 West Chester Pike, Edgemont, PA 19028

Introduction © 1986 by Harold Bloom

Printed and bound in the United States of America

∞ The paper used in this publication meets the minimum
requirements of the American National Standard for Permanence of
Paper for Printed Library Materials, Z39.48–1984.

Library of Congress Cataloging-in-Publication Data

Jonathan Swift.

    (Modern critical views)
    Bibliography: p.
    Includes index.
    Summary: A collection of critical essays on Swift
and his work. Also includes a chronology of events
in his life.
    1. Swift, Jonathan, 1667–1745—Criticism and
interpretation. [1. Swift, Jonathan, 1667–1745—
Criticism and interpretation. 2. English literature—
History and criticism] I. Bloom, Harold. II. Series.
PR3727.J626   1986b   828'.509   86–12971
ISBN 0–87754–681–9 (alk. paper)

Contents

Editor's Note

This volume gathers together a representative selection of the best criticism devoted to the writings of Jonathan Swift, the foremost ironist and satirist in the language, during the past quarter-century, reprinted here in the chronological order of its original publication. I am grateful to Christina Büchmann for her erudition and judgment in helping me choose the essays that make up this book.

The introduction centers on *A Tale of a Tub* and *Gulliver's Travels*, Swift's two masterworks, analyzing Swift's own relation both to the Tale-teller and to Gulliver. Kathleen Williams, emphasizing *The Battle of the Books*, reads the fable of the bee and the spider as a Swiftian allegory of how difficult it is to achieve order in the chaos of our fallen world, while Robert C. Elliott, meditating upon Gulliver's alienation, sees poor Gulliver as a deliberate type of comic absurdity. In a rugged exegesis of *A Tale of a Tub*, Ronald Paulson shrewdly notes that the text's tonal complexity stems from the reader's inability either to believe or reject the fiction being proposed throughout.

Martin Price, Swift's foremost critic, in this editor's judgment, sketches an outline of the ironist's formidable sense of the proper moral obligations for humankind. Swift's general view of the paradox of mankind, obscenely ridiculous yet capable of moral dignity, is surveyed by Paul Fussell in the context of Dr. Samuel Johnson's more temperate vision. A parallel contextualization, by Claude Rawson, juxtaposes Swift to Johnson but also to Alexander Pope, in regard to the stance of the relation of moral satire to its proper subject, which is not Augustan culture but the nature of man. Reflecting further upon satire, Patricia Meyer Spacks reads the *Modest Proposal* as a reminder that Swift's concerns are after all humane, even as they purport to be primarily reasonable.

Reflecting upon Gulliver among the Houyhnhnms, Peter Steele illuminatingly concludes by associating the cosmos of the fourth voyage with Samuel Beckett's *Waiting for Godot*. In another consideration of the *Modest Proposal*, David Nokes comments on the tract's relation to the terrible social conditions of Swift's Ireland. In conclusion, the issue of Swift's misogyny is placed by the feminist critic Susan Gubar in its proper context of the mythology of "the female monster" throughout Augustan satire, a placement which Ellen Pollak partly disputes by arguing that political and social factors, rather than myth, account for this aspect of eighteenth-century literature. Replying to Pollak, Gubar again maintains that the mythology she describes is prevalent not only in Augustan satire but in every period and genre of Western literature dominated by what Gertrude Stein so pungently termed "Patriarchal Poetry."

Introduction

Twice a year, for many years now, I reread Swift's *A Tale of a Tub*, not because I judge it to be the most powerful prose work in the language (which it is) but because it is good for me, though I dislike this great book as much as I admire it. A literary critic who is speculative, Gnostic, still imbued with High Romantic enthusiasm even in his later middle age, needs to read *A Tale of a Tub* as often as he can bear to do so. Swift is the most savage and merciless satirist and ironist in the history of Western literature, and one of his particularly favorite victims is the critic given to Gnostic speculations and Romantic enthusiasms.

A Tale of a Tub is a queerly shaped work, by design a parody of the seventeenth-century "anatomy," as exemplified by Sir Thomas Browne's *Pseudodoxia Epidemica* or Robert Burton's magnificent *The Anatomy of Melancholy*. The most important section of the *Tale* outrageously is not even part of the book, but is the attached fragment, *A Discourse Concerning the Mechanical Operation of the Spirit*. The philosopher Descartes, one of the leaders of the Bowmen among the Moderns in their confrontation with the Ancients in Swift's *The Battle of the Books*, is the inventor of the dualism that always will haunt the West, a dualism called "the Ghost in the Machine" by the analytical philosopher, Gilbert Ryle, and more grimly named *The Mechanical Operation of the Spirit* by Jonathan Swift. In *The Battle of the Books*, Descartes expiates his radical dualism by dying of an Aristotelian arrow intended for Bacon:

> Then *Aristotle* observing Bacon advance with a furious Mien, drew
> his Bow to the Head, and let fly his Arrow, which mist the valiant
> *Modern*, and went hizzing over his Head; but *Des-Cartes* it hit; The
> Steel Point quickly found a *Defect* in his *Head-piece*; it pierced the
> Leather and the Past-board, and went in at his Right Eye. The Tor-
> ture of the Pain, whirled the valiant *Bow-man* round, till Death, like
> a Star of superior Influence, drew him into his own *Vortex*.

Not even the dignity of an heroic death is granted to poor Descartes, who pays for his cognitive defect and perishes via an anti-Baconian shaft, swallowed

1

up into a vortex that parodies his own account of perception. Yet even this poor fate is better than the extraordinarily ferocious drubbing received by the Cartesian dualism in *The Mechanical Operation of the Spirit*:

> But, if this Plant has found a Root in the Fields of *Empire*, and of *Knowledge*, it has fixt deeper, and spread yet farther upon *Holy Ground*. Wherein, though it hath pass'd under the general Name of *Enthusiasm*, and perhaps arisen from the same Original, yet hath it produced certain Branches of a very different Nature, however often mistaken for each other. The Word in its universal Acceptation, may be defined, *A lifting up of the Soul or its Faculties above Matter*. This Description will hold good in general; but I am only to understand it, as applied to *Religion*; wherein there are three general Ways of ejaculating the Soul, or transporting it beyond the Sphere of Matter. The first, is the immediate Act of God, and is called, *Prophecy* or *Inspiration*. The second, is the immediate Act of the Devil, and is termed *Possession*. The third, is the Product of natural Causes, the effect of strong Imagination, Spleen, violent Anger, Fear, Grief, Pain, and the like. These three have been abundantly treated on by Authors, and therefore shall not employ my Enquiry. But, the fourth Method of *Religious Enthusiasm*, or launching out of the Soul, as it is purely an Effect of Artifice and *Mechanick Operation*, has been sparingly handled, or not at all, by any Writer; because tho' it is an Art of great Antiquity, yet having been confined to few Persons, it long wanted those Advancements and Refinements, which it afterwards met with, since it has grown so Epidemick, and fallen into so many cultivating Hands.

All four "methods" reduce the spirit or soul to a gaseous vapor, the only status possible for any transcendental entity in the cosmos of Hobbes and Descartes, where the soul must be ejaculated in sublime transport "beyond the Sphere of Matter." Within *A Tale of a Tub* proper, Swift keeps a very precarious balance indeed as he plays obsessively with the image of the spirit mechanically operated. So operated, the wretched soul is capable of only one mode of movement: digression. What Freud called the drive is to Swift merely digression. Digression is a turning aside, a kind of walking in which you never go straight. Digress enough, in discourse or in living, and you will go mad. *A Tale of a Tub* is nothing but digression, because Swift bitterly believes there is nothing else in a Cartesian universe. Spirit digressing is an oxymoronic operation, and so falls from spirit to gaseous vapor. Vapor properly moves only by turning aside, by digressing.

Swift's principal victims, all high priests of digression, he calls "the Learned

Aeolists," acolytes of the god of the winds, among whom he counts: "All Pretenders to Inspiration whatsoever." His savage indignation, so constant in him as a writer, maintains a consistent fury whenever the *Aeolists* are his subject. They are introduced as apocalyptics for whom origin and end intermix:

> The Learned *Aeolists*, maintain the Original Cause of all Things to be *Wind*, from which Principle this whole Universe was at first produced, and into which it must at last be resolved; that the same Breath which had kindled, and blew *up* the Flame of Nature, should one Day blow it *out*.

As he is kindled by the Aeolists, Swift's Tale-teller mounts to an intensity worthy of his subject, and attains an irony that is itself a kind of hysteria:

> It is from this Custom of the Priests, that some Authors maintain these *Aeolists*, to have been very antient in the World. Because, the Delivery of their Mysteries, which I have just now mention'd, appears exactly the same with that of other antient Oracles, whose Inspirations were owing to certain subterraneous *Effluviums of Wind*, delivered with the same Pain to the Priest, and much about the *same* Influence on the People. It is true indeed, that these were frequently managed and directed by *Female* Officers, whose Organs were understood to be better disposed for the Admission of those Oracular *Gusts*, as entring and passing up thro' a Receptacle of greater Capacity, and causing also a Pruriency by the Way, such as with due Management, hath been refined from a Carnal, into a Spiritual Extasie. And to strengthen this profound Conjecture, it is farther insisted, that this Custom of *Female* Priests is kept up still in certain refined Colleges of our *Modern Aeolists*, who are agreed to receive their Inspiration, derived thro' the Receptacle aforesaid, like their Ancestors, the *Sibyls*.

This ends in a passing blow at the Quakers, but its power is dangerously close to its horror of becoming what it is working so hard to reject. Rather like King Lear, the Tale-teller fears the ascent of vapors from abdomen to head, fears that hysteria, the womb or mother, will unman him:

> O how this mother swells up toward my heart!
> *Hysterica passio*, down, thou climbing sorrow,
> Thy element's below. —

Swift cannot be, does not want to be, the Tale-teller, but the Tale-teller may be, in part, Swift's failed defense against the madness of digression, and the digressiveness that is madness. Compulsiveness of and in the Tale-teller becomes a terrifying counter-Sublime of counter-Enthusiasm, a digressiveness turned against digressiveness, a vapor against vapors:

> Besides, there is something Individual in human Minds, that easily kindles at the accidental Approach and Collision of certain Circumstances, which tho' of paltry and mean Appearance, do often flame out into the greatest Emergencies of Life. For great Turns are not always given by strong Hands, but by lucky Adaption, and at proper Seasons; and it is of no import, where the Fire was kindled, if the Vapor has once got up into the Brain. For the *upper Region* of Man, is furnished like the *middle Region* of the Air; The Materials are formed from Causes of the widest Difference, yet produce at last the same Substance and Effect. Mists arise from the Earth, Steams from Dunghils, Exhalations from the Sea, and Smoak from Fire; yet all Clouds are the same in Composition, as well as Consequences: and the Fumes issuing from a Jakes, will furnish as comely and useful a Vapor, as Incense from an Altar. Thus far, I suppose, will easily be granted me; and then it will follow, that as the Face of Nature never produces Rain, but when it is overcast and disturbed, so Human Understanding, seated in the Brain, must be troubled and overspread by Vapours, ascending from the lower Faculties, to water the Invention, and render it fruitful.

Are these the accents of satire? The passage itself is overcast and disturbed, not so much troubled and overspread by vapors ascending from below, as it is by the not wholly repressed anxiety that *anyone*, including the Tale-teller and Swift, is vulnerable to the Mechanical Operation of the Spirit. King Henry IV of France (Henry of Navarre), rightly called "the Great," is the subject of the next paragraph, which tells of grand preparations for battle, perhaps to advance "a Scheme for Universal Monarchy," until the assassination of Henry IV released the spirit or mighty vapor from the royal body:

> Now, is the Reader exceeding curious to learn, from whence this *Vapour* took its Rise, which had so long set the Nations at a Gaze? What secret Wheel, what hidden Spring could put into Motion so wonderful an Engine? It was afterwards discovered, that the Movement of this whole Machine had been directed by an absent *Female*, whose Eyes had raised a Protuberancy, and before Emission, she was removed into an Enemy's Country. What should an unhappy Prince do in such ticklish Circumstances as these?

What indeed? This is genial, and quite relaxed, for Swift, but his subsequent analysis is darker, rhetorically and in moral substance:

Having to no purpose used all peaceable Endeavours, the collected part of the *Semen*, raised and enflamed, became adust, converted to Choler, turned head upon the spinal Duct, and ascended to the Brain. The very same Principle that influences a *Bully* to break the Windows of a Whore, who has jilted him, naturally stirs up a Great Prince to raise mighty Armies, and dream of nothing but Sieges, Battles, and Victories.

As a reduction, this continues to have its exuberance, but the phrase, "raised and enflamed" is at the center, and is yet another Swiftian assault upon Enthusiasm, another classical irony set against a romantic Sublime. The Author or Tale-teller forsakes digressiveness to become Swift at his calmest and most deadly, a transformation itself digressive. Swift cannot be censured for wanting it every which way, since he is battling not for our right reason, but for our sanity, and ruggedly he fights for us, against us, and for himself, against himself.

II

The terrible greatness of *A Tale of a Tub* has much to do with our sense of its excess, with its force being so exuberantly beyond its form (or its calculated formlessness). *Gulliver's Travels*, the later and lesser work, has survived for the common reader, whereas Swift's early masterpiece has not. Like its descendant, Carlyle's *Sartor Resartus*, *A Tale of a Tub* demands too much of the reader, but it more than rewards those demands, and it now seems unclear whether *Sartor Resartus* does or not. Gulliver's first two voyages are loved by children (of all ages), while the third and fourth voyages, being more clearly by the Swift who wrote *A Tale of a Tub*, now make their appeal only to those who would benefit most from an immersion in the *Tub*.

Gulliver himself is both the strength and the weakness of the book, and his character is particularly ambiguous in the great fourth voyage, to the country of the rational Houyhnhnms and the bestial Yahoos, who are and are not, respectively, horses and humans. The inability to resist a societal perspectivism is at once Gulliver's true weakness, and his curious strength as an observer. Swift's barely concealed apprehension that the self is an abyss, that the ego is a fiction masking our fundamental nothingness, is exemplified by Gulliver, but on a level of commonplaceness far more bathetic than anything reductive in the Tale-teller. Poor Gulliver is a good enough man, but almost devoid of imagination. One way of describing him might be to name him the least Nietzschean character ever to appear in any narrative. Though a ceaseless traveler, Gulliver lacks any desire to be elsewhere, or to be different. His pride is blind, and all too easily magnifies to pomposity, or declines to a self-contempt that is more truly a contempt for all other humans. If the Tale-teller is a Swiftian parody of one side of Swift, the anti-Cartesian, anti-Hobbesian, then Gulliver is a Swiftian parody of the great ironist's own misanthropy.

The reader of "A Voyage to Lilliput" is unlikely to forget the fatuity of Gulliver at the close of chapter 6:

> I am here obliged to vindicate the Reputation of an excellent Lady, who was an innocent Sufferer upon my Account. The Treasurer took a Fancy to be jealous of his Wife, from the Malice of some evil Tongues, who informed him that her Grace had taken a violent Affection for my Person; and the Court-Scandal ran for some Time that she once came privately to my Lodging. This I solemnly declare to be a most infamous Falshood, without any Grounds, farther than that her Grace was pleased to treat me with all innocent Marks of Freedom and Friendship. I own she came often to my House, but always publickly . . . I should not have dwelt so long upon this Particular, if it had been a Point wherein the Reputation of a great Lady is so nearly concerned, to say nothing of my own; although I had the Honour to be a *Nardac*, which the Treasurer himself is not; for all the World knows he is only a *Clumglum*, a Title inferior by one Degree, as that of a Marquess is to a Duke in *England*; yet I allow he preceded me in right of his Post.

The great *Nardac* has so fallen into the societal perspective of Lilliput, that he sublimely forgets he is twelve times the size of the *Clumglum*'s virtuous wife, who therefore would have been quite safe with him were they naked and alone. Escaping back to England, Gulliver has learned nothing and sets forth on "A Voyage to Brobdingnag," land of the giants, where he learns less than nothing:

> The Learning of this People is very defective; consisting only in Morality, History, Poetry and Mathematicks; wherein they must be allowed to excel. But, the last of these is wholly applied to what may be useful in Life; to the Improvement of Agriculture and all mechanical Arts; so that among us it would be little esteemed. And as to Ideas, Entities, Abstractions and Transcendentals, I could never drive the least Conception into their Heads.
>
> No Law of that Country must exceed in Words the Number of Letters in their Alphabet; which consists only of two and twenty. But indeed, few of them extend even to that Length. They are expressed in the most plain and simple Terms, wherein those People are not Mercurial enough to discover above one Interpretation. And, to write a Comment upon any Law, is a capital Crime. As to the Decision of

civil Causes, or Proceedings against Criminals, their Precedents are
so few, that they have little Reason to boast of any extraordinary
Skill in either.

Effective as this is, it seems too weak an irony for Swift, and we are pleased
when the dull Gulliver abandons Brobdingnag behind him. The Third Voyage,
more properly Swiftian, takes us first to Laputa, the floating island, at once a
parody of a Platonic academy yet also a kind of science fiction punishment
machine, always ready to crush earthlings who might assert liberty:

> If any Town should engage in Rebellion or Mutiny, fall into violent
> Factions, or refuse to pay the usual Tribute; the King hath two Meth-
> ods of reducing them to Obedience. The first and the mildest Course
> is by keeping the Island hovering over such a Town, and the Lands
> about it; whereby he can deprive them of the Benefit of the Sun and
> the Rain, and consequently afflict the Inhabitants with Dearth and
> Diseases. And if the Crime deserve it, they are at the same time pelted
> from above with great Stones, against which they have no Defence,
> but by creeping into Cellars or Caves, while the Roofs of their Houses
> are beaten to Pieces. But if they still continue obstinate, or offer to
> raise Insurrections; he proceeds to the last Remedy, by letting the
> Island drop directly upon their Heads, which makes a universal De-
> struction both of Houses and Men. However, this is an Extremity to
> which the Prince is seldom driven, neither indeed is he willing to put
> it in Execution; nor dare his Ministers advise him to an Action, which
> as it would render them odious to the People, so it would be a great
> Damage to their own Estates that lie all below; for the Island is the
> King's Demesn.

The maddening lack of affect on Gulliver's part begins to tell upon us here;
the stolid narrator is absurdly inadequate to the grim force of his own recital,
grimmer for us now even than it could have been for the prophetic Swift. Gulliver
inexorably and blandly goes on to *Lagado*, where he observes the grand Academy
of Projectors, Swift's famous spoof of the British Royal Society, but here the
ironies go curiously flat, and I suspect we are left with the irony of irony, which
wearies because by repetition it seems to become compulsive. Yet it may be that
here, as subsequently with the immortal but senile and noxious *Struldbruggs*, the
irony of irony is highly deliberate, in order to prepare Gulliver, and the battered
reader, for the great shock of reversal that lies just ahead in the Country of the
Houyhnhnms, which is also the land of the Yahoos, "a strange Sort of Animal."
    Critical reactions to Gulliver's fourth voyage have an astonishing range, from
Thackeray calling its moral "horrible, shameful unmanly, blasphemous" to T. S.

Eliot regarding it as a grand triumph for the human spirit. Eliot's judgment seems to me as odd as Thackeray's, and presumably both writers believed that the Yahoos were intended as a just representation of the natural man, with Thackeray humanistically disagreeing, and the neo-Christian Eliot all too happy to concur. If that were the proper reading of Swift, we would have to conclude that the great satirist had drowned in his own misanthropy, and had suffered the terrible irony, after just evading the becoming one with his Tale-teller, of joining himself to the uneducable Gulliver. Fit retribution perhaps, but it is unwise to underestimate the deep cunning of Swift.

Martin Price accurately reminds us that Swift's attitudes do not depend solely upon Christian morals, but stem also from a traditional secular wisdom. Peace and decency are wholly compatible with Christian teaching, but are secular virtues as well. Whatever the Yahoos represent, they are *not* a vision of secular humanity devoid of divine grace, since they offend the classical view of man quite as profoundly as they seem to suit an ascetic horror of our supposedly natural condition.

Clearly, it is the virtues of the Houyhnhnms, and not the squalors of the Yahoos, that constitute a burden for critics and for common readers. I myself agree with Price, when he remarks of the Houyhnhnms: "They are rational horses, neither ideal men nor a satire upon others' ideals for man." Certainly they cannot represent a human rational ideal, since none of us would wish to lack all impulse, or any imagination whatsoever. Nor do they seem a plausible satire upon the Deistic vision, a satire worthier of Blake than of Swift, and in any case contradicted by everything that truly is admirable about these cognitively advanced horses. A rational horse is a kind of oxymoron, and Swift's irony is therefore more difficult than ever to interpret:

> My Master heard me with great Appearances of Uneasiness in his Countenance; because *Doubting* or *not believing*, are so little known in this Country, that the Inhabitants cannot tell how to behave themselves under such Circumstances. And I remember in frequent Discourses with my Master concerning the Nature of Manhood, in other Parts of the World; having Occasion to talk of *Lying*, and *false Representation*, it was with much Difficulty that he comprehended what I meant; although he had otherwise a most acute Judgment. For he argued thus; That the Use of Speech was to make us understand one another, and to receive Information of Facts; now if any one *said the Thing which was not*, these Ends were defeated; because I cannot properly be said to understand him; and I am so far from receiving Information, that he leaves me worse than in Ignorance; for I am led to believe a Thing *Black* when it is *White*, and *Short* when it is

Long. And these were all the Notions he had concerning the Faculty of *Lying*, so perfectly well understood, and so universally practised among human Creatures.

Are we altogether to admire Gulliver's Master here, when that noble Houyhnhnm not only does not know how to react to the human propensity to say *the thing which was not*, but lacks even the minimal imagination that might allow him to apprehend the human need for fictions, a "sickness not ignoble," as Keats observed in *The Fall of Hyperion*? Since the noble Houyhnhnm finds the notion "that the *Yahoos* were the only governing Animals" in Gulliver's country "altogether past his Conception," are we again to admire him for an inability that would make it impossible for us to read *Gulliver's Travels* (or *King Lear*, for that matter)? The virtues of Swift's rational horses would not take us very far, if we imported them into our condition, but can that really be one of Swift's meanings? And what are we to do with Swiftian ironies that are too overt already, and become aesthetically intolerable if we take up the stance of the sublimely rational Houyhnhnm?

> My Master likewise mentioned another Quality, which his Servants had discovered in several *Yahoos*, and to him was wholly unaccountable. He said, a Fancy would sometimes take a *Yahoo*, to retire into a Corner, to lie down and howl, and groan, and spurn away all that came near him, although he were young and fat, and wanted neither Food nor Water; nor did the Servants imagine what could possibly ail him. And the only Remedy they found was to set him to hard Work, after which he would infallibly come to himself. To this I was silent out of Partiality to my own Kind; yet here I could plainly discover the true Seeds of *Spleen*, which only seizeth on the *Lazy*, the *Luxurious*, and the *Rich*; who, if they were forced to undergo the *same Regimen*, I would undertake for the Cure.
>
> His Honour had farther observed, that a Female-*Yahoo* would often stand behind a Bank or a Bush, to gaze on the young Males passing by, and then appear, and hide, using many antick Gestures and Grimaces; at which time it was observed, that she had a most *offensive Smell*; and when any of the Males advanced, would slowly retire, looking often back, and with a counterfeit Shew of Fear, run off into some convenient Place where she knew the Male would follow her.

Swift rather dubiously seems to want it every which way at once, so that the Yahoos both are and are not representations of ourselves, and the Houyhnhnms are and are not wholly admirable or ideal. Or is it the nature of irony itself, which must weary us, or finally make us long for a true sublime, even if it should turn out to be grotesque? Fearfully strong writer that he was, Swift as ironist resembles Kafka far more than say Orwell, among modern authors. We do not know precisely how to read "In the Penal Colony" or *The Trial*, and we certainly do not know exactly how to interpret Gulliver's fourth voyage. What most merits interpretation in Kafka is the extraordinary perversity of imagination with which he so deliberately makes himself uninterpretable. Is Swift a similar problem for the reader? What is the proper response to the dismaying conclusion of *Gulliver's Travels*?

> Having thus answered the *only* Objection that can be raised against me as a Traveller; I here take a final Leave of my Courteous Readers, and return to enjoy my own Speculations in my little Garden at *Redriff*; to apply those excellent Lessons of Virtue which I learned among the *Houyhnhms*; to instruct the *Yahoos* of my own Family as far as I shall find them docible Animals; to behold my Figure often in a Glass, and thus if possible habituate my self by Time to tolerate the Sight of a human Creature: To lament the Brutality of *Houyhnhms* in my own Country, but always treat their Persons with Respect, for the Sake of my noble Master, his Family, his Friends, and the whole *Houyhnhnm* Race, whom these of ours have the Honour to resemble in all their Lineaments, however their Intellectuals came to degenerate.
>
> I began last Week to permit my Wife to sit at Dinner with me, at the Farthest End of a long Table; and to answer (but with the utmost Brevity) the few Questions I ask her. Yet the Smell of a *Yahoo* continuing very offensive, I always keep my Nose well stopt with Rue, Lavender, or Tobacco-Leaves. And although it be hard for a Man late in Life to remove old Habits; I am not altogether out of Hopes in some Time to suffer a Neighbour *Yahoo* in my Company, without the Apprehensions I am yet under of his Teeth or his Claws.

Who are those "Courteous Readers" of whom Gulliver takes his final leave here? We pity the poor fellow, but we do not so much pity Mrs. Gulliver as wonder how she can tolerate the insufferable wretch. Yet the final paragraphs have a continued power that justifies their fame, even as we continue to see Gulliver as deranged:

> My Reconcilement to the *Yahoo*-kind in general might not be so difficult, if they would be content with those Vices and Follies only which Nature hath entitled them to. I am not in the least provoked at the Sight of a Lawyer, a Pick-pocket, a Colonel, a Fool, a Lord, a Gamster, a Politician, a Whoremunger, a Physician, an Evidence, a

Suborner, an Attorney, a Traytor, or the like: This is all according to
the due Course of Things: But, when I behold a Lump of Deformity,
and Diseases both in Body and Mind, smitten with *Pride*, it immediately breaks all the Measures of my Patience; neither shall I be ever
able to comprehend how such an Animal and such a Vice could tally
together. The wise and virtuous *Houyhnhnms*, who abound in all
Excellencies that can adorn a rational Creature, have no Name for this
Vice in their Language, whereby they describe the detestable Qualities
of their *Yahoos*; among which they were not able to distinguish this
of Pride, for want of thoroughly understanding Human Nature, as
it sheweth it self in other Countries, where that Animal presides. But
I, who had more Experience, could plainly observe some Rudiments
of it among the wild *Yahoos*.

But the *Houyhnhnms*, who live under the Government of Reason,
are no more proud of the good Qualities they possess, than I should
be for not wanting a Leg or an Arm, which no Man in his Wits
would boast of, although he must be miserable without them. I dwell
the longer upon this Subject from the Desire I have to make the
Society of an *English Yahoo* by any Means not insupportable; and
therefore I here intreat those who have any Tincture of this absurd
Vice, that they will not presume to appear in my Sight.

What takes precedence here, the palpable hit at the obscenity of false human pride, or the madness of Gulliver, who thinks he is a Yahoo, longs to be a
Houyhnhnm, and could not bear to be convinced that he is neither? As in *A Tale
of a Tub*, Swift audaciously plays at the farthest limits of irony, limits that make
satire impossible, because no norm exists to which we might hope to return.

KATHLEEN WILLIAMS

Giddy Circumstance

It has been the purpose of the preceding chapters to suggest that Swift, both by nature and by reason of the confused and transitional age in which he lived, was disposed to see the conditions of human life as chaotic and difficult. Desiring the order and unity and simplicity of traditional aspiration, he saw little hope of attaining it in man's world of deceit, and the ways of achieving order that were being tried in his lifetime could only succeed by leaving out half the truth about man and his world. Faced by extreme philosophies, extreme moral and political systems, each with its own neat little parody of completeness, Swift assumes a position between them, follows the middle way which will allow him to take advantage of the partial truths on either side and to drop what seems to him valueless. This necessity affects the form and the content of his satires alike. Swift is one of the most difficult writers of the very allusive and complicated satire of the seventeenth and eighteenth centuries because he is trying to perform a particularly difficult task. For the problems which he saw, there could be only a tentative and partial solution: he is concerned to hold the precarious balance of a traditional view of man, his nature, his relation to his fellows, his God, and the world about him, in conditions increasingly hostile to it. To know that truth exists, but to acknowledge the difficulty of attaining it, to weigh the claims of mind and body, of eternal truth and inescapable "circumstance," was to be assailed from all sides. Extreme rationalism and enthusiasm, the determined optimism of Shaftesbury and the cynicism of Mandeville, all these divergent attitudes were in some way upsetting the balance, oversimplifying the complex and

From *Jonathan Swift and the Age of Compromise.* © 1958 by the University of Kansas Press.

difficult reality and so moving further into the dangers of deception, making still harder the lot of man struggling to know himself and such truth as he may grasp. Swift's satire, consequently, is of a very complicated kind, for the extremes which he attacks are aberrations from a norm which is itself a compromise difficult to express in positive terms and existing in avoidance of error, that error of stressing one aspect of the human situation to the detriment of the rest which is perhaps best summed up in Swift's own neat comment upon the Stoics: "The Stoical Scheme of supplying our Wants, by lopping off our Desires; is like cutting off our Feet when we want Shoes."

In most of the problems which he presents to us in his satiric and other writing, Swift's solution is, then, necessarily one of compromise. At worst, in the realm of practical politics for instance, this is an uneasy balance of forces; at best, as in *Gulliver's Travels*, a true reconciliation by which essential yet apparently opposed truths can be brought together. Such a reconciliation can only be expressed by a complexity of method which is Swift's equivalent of the seventeenth-century literature of paradox and the eighteenth-century literature of antithesis. In government there must be a balance of power between king and aristocracy and people, while for the individual the best way is to avoid the harmful extremes of either party, Whig or Tory. As for the morality of the state, again Swift sees the solution in a middle way: the state, concerned with its schemes of wealth and power, cannot be a truly moral entity, but it can help and encourage virtue, even if its motives in doing so are not of the highest, and the "particular person" in his relation to the state can help both it and himself by honesty. But behind all these lesser compromises lies the fundamental compromise of man himself; man the creature of self-love whose passions lead him astray but who yet, if he recognizes and uses these passions, may become more actively and usefully and fully virtuous than the passionless Stoic can ever be; man who is no longer innocent but can become good if he recognizes himself for what he is. At the heart of all Swift's writing is the animal, man; all his problems and solutions are related to his strong sense of the complexity of our nature, "the best and worst that may be had," and of the necessity of somehow reconciling passion and reason, body and mind, to reach the kind of goodness attainable by, and proper to, so mixed and limited a creature. Perhaps in no writer do we feel more strongly the insistent presence of humanity. As moralist, preacher, political theorist, Swift is never abstract. Always the "particular person"—the honest trader, the humble listener in the congregation, the apparent author or the apparent audience—gives vividness and actuality to his words; always we feel ourselves in touch with a human being, always with Swift himself in his humor and affection, his angry compassion, his desire to be of practical use, and intermittently with his narrators, stupid, complacent, well-meaning, or urbane. In each case, we have to deal not with ideas only, but with ideas as they are formulated by a person with all his oddities, vanities, "prejudices," indignations; not with mind only, but with that mixture of mental activity with bodily impulses which makes up the animal capable of reason. Swift's impatience of "Ideas, Entities, Abstractions and Transcendentals" is everywhere obvious; he is not interested in theories or systems except as they affect or are affected by John, Peter, and Thomas. No system can long survive unchanged when it has to take its chance with unpredictable mankind, and most ineffective of all are the systems which try to schematize man himself. Only revealed religion can account for man, and the Christian view is one which allows full value to his complexity.

This preoccupation with man is to be felt in all Swift's work, satiric or not, but in the satires it is overwhelmingly strong. Satire, of course, must be concerned with human beings, but Swift's major satires are concerned with humanity at a deeper level than that of individual oddities or wickedness. He investigates, rather, the nature of man from which behavior arises, and criticizes those philosophies and systems which are based on a misunderstanding of that nature. People of all kinds throng his pages, contributing to his investigation; giants and pygmies, ancients and moderns, Gulliver and Bentley and the author of *A Tale of a Tub*, and whether or not they are presented as consistent characters each one of them is, at each given moment, a most convincing representative of confused humanity. For it is the complexity of man's nature which is Swift's chief point; complexity, inconsistency, fallibility, the variousness of his self-deceit, and the humility and effort which are necessary if he is to grow into the kind of goodness possible to him. By indirection, by ridicule of false extremes and simplifications, the positive is implied, and the positive is the traditional Renaissance view of man as a limited creature in whom mind and body are at odds and must be, as far as possible, reconciled. Swift said of his poetry, light though much of it seems, that he wrote no line "without a moral view," and this is even more true of the great prose satires. Even *The Battle of the Books*, starting from the literary argument in which Sir William Temple had so unfortunately involved himself, has behind it a firm conception of the nature of man, and from the *Battle* and the *Tale* to *Gulliver's Travels* this conception is essentially unchanged, though experience strengthened and deepened it. *A Tale of a Tub*, the "young man's book," is a brilliant presentation of the predicament of man on his isthmus of middle state, and of the absurdity of his attempts to better himself, though its very brilliance does in a way obscure the central conception on which the book is based, because we are conscious chiefly of a dazzling intellectual activity on the part of Swift himself as he shifts and maneuvers to display all the varying absurdities he wishes to satirize. It is mind in all its pride and energy that we feel in *A Tale of a Tub*; yet what the book is primarily about is the weakness of mind, so easily governed by bodily desires or diseases, by vanity or self-interest, or by the deceit of the senses. The point is made most clearly in the case of the Aeolists, or the great conquerors, whose mental activity is caused by, and warped by, the merest physical accident. But both for Swift and for his readers, through most of the *Tale*, this truth is as yet a matter of intellectual acceptance and intellectual enjoyment, rather than of experience. What is constantly in Swift's mind is the glorious absurdity of man's pompous claims and of his blindness to his predicament; he is less concerned, in this youthful work, with the predicament itself, though that underlies all the ridiculousness of the Aeolists and of the "modern" author. But in *Gulliver's Travels* the human situation has been deeply felt and painfully experienced, and the technique as well as the attitude has matured. Here body as well as mind is constantly, even oppressively, present; no longer can the intellect range freely in wild parodies of speculation, but is caught in the minuscule bodies of Lilliput or in the clumsy bodies of Brobdingnag, and in each case obviously and inescapably influenced by the body in which it dwells. In *A Tale of a Tub*, the paradox of man is posed and contemplated, a source of laughter and delight: in *Gulliver's Travels* the two sides of man's nature are kept gravely before us, forcing us to experience for ourselves, as never in the *Tale*, the inexorability of the human situation. And when we are sufficiently convinced, sufficiently resigned, a solution—the only solution possible for Swift—is unobtrusively suggested. Sublunary chaos, giddy circumstance, is no longer simply displayed, however delightfully; through Gulliver and the varied creatures he meets on his travels, chaos is grasped and ordered, so far as man can order it.

The Battle of the Books is perhaps the least interesting, as well as the least characteristic, of Swift's longer satires, and for that reason may be first considered, though parts at least of *A Tale of a Tub* were written earlier. It has an air of real detachment—as distinct from the assumed detachment of *A Modest Proposal*—which is unusual in him. He makes the satirist's formal pretense to impartiality: "I, being possessed of all Qualifications requisite in an Historian, and retained by neither Party; have resolved to comply with the urgent Importunity of my Friends, by writing down a full impartial Account thereof." The joke here is that we are supposed to see at once how exceedingly partial the author is, though he is only writing, as so many claimed to be, through the "urgent Importunity" of his friends, and of course it is plain enough from the outset that the *Battle* is a blow on behalf of the ancients and of their supporters, chiefly Boyle and Sir William Temple, who are represented as honorary ancients. But as we read on, the ironic claim begins to seem almost a double bluff, for though Swift has chosen his side and believes he has chosen rightly, he seems not very deeply concerned in the matter. The actual battle, led on one side by the formidable combination of Homer, Pindar, Euclid, Plato, Aristotle, Herodotus, Livy, and Hippocrates, and on the other by a rabble of contenders for the chief command, is a lighthearted affair in which Swift's interest, and ours, lies not so much in the rights and wrongs of the argument as in the fun of the parody of heroic language and incidents and in the ingenuity of the episodes. The exchange of armor and the projected exchange of horses between Virgil and Dryden, or Wotton's abortive attack on Temple, who "neither felt the Weapon touch him, nor heard it fall," and indeed most of the contests, are amusing and neat in their translation of literary differences into physical encounters, but the ingenuity is the thing here, as in Pope's hilarious heroic games in *The Dunciad*. Swift was not by nature disposed to see things in plain black and white; perhaps the issue here, necessarily prejudged for him as a supporter of Temple against the well-armored Bentley, was too simplified to be real, and made too little appeal for him to feel deeply involved, though his admiration for Temple and the life that Temple stood for was real enough. In his later work he does not show himself ready to applaud or condemn either party without reservations, and even here several of the moderns are courteously treated, Cowley, Denham, Milton (whom Swift certainly admired), and, notably, Bacon, among them.

The satiric method, too, seems almost groping, considering the apparent ease and confidence with which the other early work, *A Tale of a Tub*, is written and shaped despite its far more complex theme. The *Battle* is clever but episodic, with allegories, parody, mock-heroic, each one neat in itself but all loosely strung together, and the satire is, for Swift, unusually simple and direct. It is not his normal habit to show his hand so plainly as he does here, with his opening allegory of the twin peaks of Parnassus and the causes of war, which are poverty and want on the part of the aggressor. As for the mock-heroic of the battle in St. James's Library, this was a mode of writing which at the end of the seventeenth century not only gave a clear warning of satiric intention but indicated pretty precisely how the satire would go; it is a far cry from this to the businesslike approach of *A Modest Proposal*, or the factual sober air of *Gulliver's Travels*. *A Modest Proposal* could, at first, be yet another in that spate of impractical suggestions for improving the state of Ireland which so wearied Swift; the *Travels* could, at first, be another adventure story or at most another version of those many voyages to the moon or to the Antipodes which the reading public had been enjoying for so many years. We discover very quickly, it is true, that neither is what it seems, but it takes us a great deal longer to discover what, exactly, it is, and the false start is part of the effect. The recognition of the full satiric intention in these works of Swift's maturity involves reorientation and a necessary concern on the part of the reader; in *The Battle of the Books* we are complacently certain at the outset of the course to be run, and our complacency is never disturbed.

Indeed, we are here in a far more solid and familiar world than the one which Swift usually prepares for our discomfiture. Both the form and the supposed author are what they seem, though in fact the author contributes little to satiric meaning. Perhaps nowhere in Swift's work is the method simpler, except in political tracts where for the moment all that is in question is attack on, or ridicule of, a particular person or policy. Indeed the situation here is similar to that in a political pamphlet; an enclosed area of human experience has to be considered, in which attitudes approximating to right and wrong may be seen and in which it is necessary to "chuse one of the two Sides, although he cannot entirely approve of either." The intention of the satire is limited, and not of a kind to inspire Swift's more characteristic effects, and the method is, consequently, comparatively uncomplicated. The author is, for the most part, a mere eyewitness, reporting what he has seen and heard; he approaches most nearly to the modern author of A Tale of a Tub in his portentous opening remarks, and in the series of ingenious analogies which prove so little and please him so much. "NOW," he says proudly, after his argument from the causes of war as seen in the Republick of Dogs, "NOW, whoever will please to take this Scheme, and either reduce or adapt it to an Intellectual State, or Commonwealth of Learning, will soon discover the first Ground of Disagreement between the two great Parties at this Time in Arms." But there is only a hint of the joyous lunacy of A Tale of a Tub in these parodies of ingenious, pointless argument; usually the parody is as straightforward as that of the "Tritical Essay," and soon we find ourselves in the Library of St. James's, watching the contest between the books in whose rival merits Swift is not deeply concerned.

But behind the rivalries of Virgil and Dryden, Cowley and Pindar, as behind the whole seventeenth-century quarrel of the ancients and the moderns, lies the larger issue of what man is capable of: the difference between those who believe that his powers are strictly limited and those who believe in his power to improve upon existing knowledge and achievement. The real importance of the quarrel in England was not literary but scientific and philosophic; and here it touches questions which were vital to Swift. One of the encounters in the battle is between Aristotle and Bacon; Aristotle shoots, but his arrow "mist the valiant Modern, and went hizzing over his Head; but Des-Cartes it hit; The Steel Point quickly found a Defect in his Head-piece; it pierced the Leather and the Pastboard, and went in at his right Eye. The Torture of the Pain, whirled the valiant Bow-man round, till Death, like a Star of superior Influence, drew him into his own Vortex." For Swift, Bacon as experimenter working humbly upon the matter of experience and as an opposer of those who domineer over nature was not unacceptable; it was Descartes, progenitor of the race of modern system-makers, who was representative of all that was presumptuous and dangerous in rationalizing modernism. James Keill, Newton's associate, sums up this attitude. Descartes, he says, has encouraged "this presumptuous pride in the Philosophers, that they think they understand all of the works of Nature, and are able to give a good account of them. . . . He was the first world-maker this Century produced, for he supposes that God at the beginning created only a certain quantity of matter, and motion, and from thence he endeavours to shew, how, by the necessary law of Mechanisme, without any extraordinary concurrence of Divine Power, the world and all that therein is might have been produced." This aspect of the quarrel is dealt with in the encounter between the Spider and the Bee, the one passage in the book in which the allegory is rich with compressed meaning. Various aspects of modern presumption are drawn together in this episode by means of allusion; it is an early example of the density which Swift can achieve in his prose, though rarely in the poetry, where one might rather expect to find it. Some of the meaning is expounded, fittingly enough, by Aesop, master of the beast fable; as he points out, the two insects have, by implication, summed up the whole situation. Indeed the uncouth and choleric spider, with his boasts of self-sufficiency, of being "furnisht with a Native Stock within my self," is an excellent symbol of the particular vice of modernism, especially since the buildings on which he prides himself constitute in fact not a "Fortress" or a "large Castle" but a cobweb, ephemeral and flimsy as the cloud embraced, in mistake for Juno, by Bishop Huet's rationalist philosophers. The elaborate structure spun from the spider's own entrails is quickly shattered by the mere presence of the bee, though it makes no deliberate attack upon the fortifications, and the bee's civilized demeanor and polished utterance as quickly shows up the barbarism and ignorance of the spider. The contrast between an urbane traditional culture, always in touch with the world about it, and the unbalanced pride of word-spinning and system-spinning modernism, could scarcely be better displayed.

Several more particular applications can be made of the episode. It is, for instance, an excellent illustration of the difference between the traditional neo-classic literary theory and the new developments which were already opposing it. The bee's description of its activity as being "That, which, by an universal Range, with long Search, much Study, true Judgment, and Distinction of Things, brings home Honey and Wax" suggests the old conception of literature as a reshaping, through the vigorous effort of the individual, of existing materials; the spider follows the easier course of a self-expression uncontrolled by reference to anything beyond himself, and so lacking in that discipline which is forced upon the bee by the effort to interpret the outside world and extract from it honey and wax, or as Aesop puts it "the two Noblest of Things, which are Sweetness and Light." Sir William Temple had used the bee as a symbol of proper creative activity in his "Essay of Poetry," referring to the art and labor, and the difficult task of judging and selecting, involved in the bee's choice of flowers, extraction of honey, and separation of the wax. But the bee and the spider belong also to those philosophical and scientific differences which were undermining the ways of thought from which classical literary theory sprang; they had been used to symbolize the quarrel between those who were content to observe and experience, and those who were óvereager to theorize. Francis Bacon had seen scholasticism as a spider, spinning useless cobwebs of learning out of little matter and infinite agitation of wit; in *Novum Organum* he compares the men of experiment with the ant, who only collects and uses, the reasoners with the spiders, "which spin webs out of their own bowels," and the true philosopher with the bee, who takes a middle course, for "she draws her materials from the flowers of the garden and the field, and yet changes and digests them by a power of her own." Bacon's middle way would no doubt appeal to Swift as an assertion of the ordering and shaping power of the mind within the limits he would regard as possible and permissible. Mind has a strenuous part to play, but a limited part; it must take into account the confusion of the world and work upon it, for though we cannot escape from chaos we can by difficult effort compose it into meaning.

The spider and the bee were, therefore, already familiar symbols when Swift wrote, and others before him had related Bacon's spider to rationalists of all kinds, Cartesian as well as scholastic. One of the most notorious of contemporary system-makers was Dr. Thomas Burnet, who a few years before had spun what was perhaps the most intricate and flimsy cobweb of all in his account of the creation and subsequent history of the world, *Telluris Theoria Sacra*. This extraordinary work was seen to be not only an unfounded hypothesis but a dangerous one, tending to the denial of the Biblical story of man's creation and fall, and taking too little account of final causes; and such de-spiritualizing of the universe was detestable to Swift as to many of his contemporaries. In the *Battle* he has a passing hit at these system-makers with their absorption in efficient causes and their failure to relate them to the Final Cause, in the passage describing the visit of Fame to Jupiter. She tells him of the impending battle, and having consulted the Book of Fate he summons a number of menial gods: "These are his ministring Instruments in all Affairs below. They travel in a Caravan, more or less together, and are fastened to each other like a Link of Gally-slaves, by a light Chain, which passes from them to Jupiter's great Toe: And yet in receiving or delivering a Message, they may never approach above the lowest Step of his Throne, where he and they whisper to each other thro' a long hollow Trunk. These Deities are call'd by mortal Men, Accidents, or Events; but the Gods call them, Second Causes." This is a lightly turned comment on the pursuers of second causes; follow the chain of causation as far as they will, there will still be an unbridgable gap between it and the final cause. They can reach no further than the lowest step of God's throne, and the divine intentions cannot be penetrated by such investigations. They will succeed only in cutting themselves off from the true understanding which can be reached by accepting the mysterious purposes of God; as Meric Casaubon put it, men who kept their minds fixed on matter and secondary causes might "forget that there be such things in the world as spirits, and at last that there is a God, and that their souls are immortal." The divine decrees become, to mankind, mere "Accidents, or Events." Mysteries must and will remain, for all the explanations given from second causes by the moderns.

It has recently been demonstrated that Swift's spider has particular reference to Burnet, who recounts an eastern legend of a cosmic spider which spun the universe and governs it as it would a web—as do the system-makers themselves—while the bee, on the other hand, is a familiar symbol of the good life, ancient and modern. Marvell's "Garden," for instance, the place of all traditional God-centered wisdom, is the home of the bee, working intelligently upon the glories of the created world, and it is the bee who closes and sums up the poem:

> Where, from above, the milder sun
> Does through a fragrant zodiac run,
> And, as it works, the industrious bee
> Computes its time, as well as we!

The contrast of bee and spider bears upon the fundamental moral problems of the age; it is not surprising that in this episode Swift's satire becomes more complex and less direct, drawing many allusions and meanings into a small space. It is more characteristic of him than is any other part of *The Battle of the Books*, and not the least typical aspect of the passage is its embodiment of theory in persons—for the insects have recognizably human personalities. One of the implicit arguments against modern theorizing is that it produces a Bentley or a Burnet-spider; one of the arguments for ancient humility is the wise bee, or the courteous and magnanimous Charles Boyle. As always, attitudes of mind are displayed through, and judged by, the results they produce in conduct. Although they are obscured by the topical jokes of the battle itself, there are important issues hinted at in this otherwise rather impersonal and, for Swift, rather unorganized and simple book. The real function of man in the world is already his main interest, and the good life with its unambitious achievement of order and meaning within the framework of traditional acceptances, is set against the fantasy world of the reasoners in their strongholds which can be broken at the first touch of reality.

ROBERT C. ELLIOTT

The Satirist Satirized

If we ask who is the satirist of *Gulliver's Travels*, the answer obviously is Swift — or, if he is not "of" *Gulliver's Travels*, he is the satirist who creates the satire of *Gulliver's Travels*. But in the extended sense of the term we are familiar with Gulliver is also a satirist, different from Timon, but in his own way as devastating:

"[I assured his Honour] That, our young *Noblemen* are bred from their Childhood in Idleness and Luxury; that, as soon as Years will permit, they consume their Vigour, and contract odious Diseases among Lewd Females; and when their Fortunes are almost ruined, they marry some Woman of mean Birth, disagreeable Person, and unsound Constitution, merely for the sake of Money, whom they hate and despise. That, the Productions of such Marriages are generally scrophulous, rickety or deformed Children; by which Means the Family seldom continues above three Generations, unless the Wife take Care to provide a healthy Father among her Neighbours, or Domesticks, in order to improve and continue the Breed. That, a weak diseased Body, a meager Countenance, and sallow Complexion, are the true Marks of *noble Blood*; and a healthy robust Appearance is so disgraceful in a Man of Quality, that the World concludes his real Father to have been a Groom or a Coachman. The Imperfections of his Mind run parallel with those of his Body; being a Composition of Spleen, Dulness, Ignorance, Caprice, Sensuality and Pride."

This of course is the Gulliver of the Fourth Voyage, worlds removed from the ship's surgeon who was charmed with the Lilliputians and quick with praise of "my own dear native Country." That Gulliver, he of the early voyages, is so far from being a satirist that he is often the butt *par excellence* of satire: Swift's satire, of course, and, within the work, the King of Brobdingnag's; but also, in a

---

From *The Power of Satire: Magic, Ritual, Art.* © 1960 by Princeton University Press.

23

sense, of his own—his, that is, when he is an old man, sitting down to unaccustomed literary labors to compose his memoirs.

We must look at some of the formal relations governing the work. Swift gives us little "outside" information about how or when Gulliver wrote the account of his travels. Richard Sympson, the fictive publisher, said to be a relative of Gulliver on his mother's side, writes that he corrected the Captain's papers; and Gulliver himself complains that his manuscript has been tampered with. That is all we know. Within the work itself, however, is evidence that Gulliver composed his memoirs as an elderly man, after he had retired from his unfortunate life on the sea. Several times in the narrative Gulliver looks back in chronological time to previous voyages, bringing his experience from them to bear on a "present" predicament; but he never looks forward specifically to "future" adventures as commentary on what is happening at the moment. Still, it is apparent from casual comments in the early voyages that a whole realm of "future" experience is available to the writer. For example, at the end of part I Gulliver describes his preparations for shipping out again: "My Daughter *Betty* (who is now well married, and has Children) was then at her Needle-Work." Between "now"—at the time of writing—and "then" lie the years of Gulliver's three subsequent voyages, plus five years which elapse between his final return to England and the composition of the work.

The Gulliver who writes, then, is Gulliver the misanthrope who stuffs his nose with tobacco leaves and keeps a long table between himself and his wife. It is he who "creates" the ship's surgeon—a man capable of longing for the tongue of Demosthenes so that he may celebrate his country in a style equal to its unparalleled merits. Given the emotional and intellectual imbalance of the old seaman, he is remarkably successful in producing an objective portrait of himself as he was in time long past.

The actual, as opposed to the fictive, situation, of course, is that Swift has created two dominant points of view to control the materials of the *Travels*: that of his favorite *ingénu* (the younger Gulliver) and that of the misanthrope. The technique has obvious advantages. An *ingénu* is a superb agent of indirect satire as he roams the world uncritically recording or even embracing the folly which it is the satirist's business to undermine: "*Flimnap*, the Treasurer, is allowed to cut a Caper on the strait Rope, at least an Inch higher than any other Lord in the whole Empire." On the other hand, a misanthrope can develop all the great power of direct, hyperbolic criticism. By allowing Gulliver, an uncritical lover of man, to become an uncritical hater of man, Swift has it both ways.

The technique is not that of the novelist, however. Swift pays little regard to psychological consistency; Gulliver's character can hardly be said to develop; it simply changes. If one takes seriously the premise that Gulliver writes his memoirs after his rebirth, then many passages in the early voyages turn out to be inconsistent and out of character. "There are," says Gulliver of Lilliput, "some Laws and Customs in this Empire very peculiar; and if they were not so directly contrary to those of my own dear Country, I should be tempted to say a little in their Justification." (The laws from Swift's point of view, from the point of view of reason, are excellent.) Here Gulliver is trapped in a conflict between his patriotism and his reason; as he is an *ingénu* his patriotism wins. But note the tense: "I should be tempted"; that is, now—at the time of writing. Given this tense, and given the logic of the controlling situation, it must follow that this is the utterance of Gulliver as he composes the work. At the time he writes, however, Gulliver is committed so irrevocably to the claims of reason that the appeal of patriotism could not possibly have meaning for him—could not, that is, if we assume general consistency in Gulliver's character.

Similar examples of what in novels would be called inconsistency in characterization can be found in nearly all Menippean satires. The first surviving sequence of the *Satyricon* is a direct, serious attack on current abuses in the teaching of oratory; the sentiments are, presumably, those of Petronius, but they are incongruously delivered through the mouth of Encolpius. Two minutes after delivering the attack, Encolpius is racing through a bawdy house where he is unquestionably more at home. There is an amusing passage in Apuleius where Lucius, still in the form of an ass, delivers a diatribe against the venality of judges: "Well, then, you lowest of the low, yes, I am referring to the whole legal profession. All you cattle-like law-clerks and vulture-like barristers—are you really surprised that modern judges are corrupt . . . ?" But then, after some ransacking of history and myth, he breaks off. "Forgive this outburst! I can hear my readers protesting: 'Hey, what's all this about? Are we going to let an ass lecture us in philosophy?' Yes, I dare say I had best return to my story." Many of the tales of *The Golden Ass*, charming in themselves, are told by the most inappropriate persons. Finally, one does not, after all, read *Brave New World* or Nathaniel West's *A Cool Million* for insight into individual human character. In all these works characters may be amusing, likable, touching—even "consistent"—but almost as by-products of their primary function. They are first of all agents of satire, and the ordinary criteria by which we judge character in novels do not apply.

On the other hand, as though to contradict the above, Menippean satire may employ techniques that we are accustomed to associate only with the most sophisticated novelists. I propose to follow Professor Auerbach's analysis of one such technique as Petronius uses it. The scene is the fantastic banquet given by the parvenu Trimalchio. Encolpius, the narrator of the *Satyricon* asks his neighbor at the table to identify the woman who is busily running up and down the banquet hall. He obliges:

"That's Trimalchio's wife. Fortunata they call her. She measures money by the bushel. Yet not so long ago, not so long ago, what was she? I hope you won't

mind my putting it that way, but you wouldn't have accepted a piece of bread
from her hands. Now she sits on top of the world and is Trimalchio's one and
only. . . . He can't keep track of what he owns; he's so filthy rich. But that bitch
looks out for everything, even where you'd least expect it. She doesn't drink;
she's level-headed; her advice is good. But she has a nasty tongue and gossips like
a magpie once she gets settled on her cushion. When she likes a person, she really
likes him. When she hates one, she certainly hates him. Trimalchio's estates reach
as far as a falcon flies. And some money he has! There's more silver in his porter's
lodge than any one man's whole estate. And the number of slaves he's got! O my
God, I don't think one out of ten knows his master even by sight. Believe me, he
could stick any of these louts here in his pocket. . . . But his fellow freedmen are
not to be despised either. They aren't badly off. Look at the one sitting all the
way back there. Today he is worth eight hundred thousand, and when he started
out he had nothing. Not so long ago he carried wood around on his back. But
they say—of course I don't know, except that I have heard people talk about it
—they say he stole a goblin's magic cap and then found a treasure. Well I won't
begrudge a fellow what God has given him. . . . That one there sitting with the
freedmen—he used to have a nicely feathered nest too. I don't want to say anything against him. He had a cool million. But somehow he slipped badly."

The response is remarkable in its circumstantiality, depicting as it does not
only Fortunata and Trimalchio and his fellow freedmen, but the values of a whole
society and, indeed, of the speaker himself. His language, full of jargon and
cliché, throws a light inward, as it were, for it reveals the speaker for what he is:
one completely and unselfconsciously at home in the milieu he describes. His
wistful awe in the face of all that money places him perfectly. Society and speaker
are finely rendered, objectified, for our view. Petronius, however, has not simply
set down an objective description of a society of freedmen, as if to say: this is the
way it was. Instead, writes Auerbach, he has given us a subjective image of the
society as it exists in the mind of a man who is himself a member of the society.

"[Petronius] lets an 'I' who is identical neither with himself nor yet with
the feigned narrator Encolpius, turn the spotlight of his perception on the company at table—a highly artful procedure in perspective, a sort of twofold mir-
roring, which I dare not say is unique in antique literature as it has come down to
us, but which is most unusual there. . . . Nowhere, except in this passage from
Petronius, do we have, on the one hand, the most intense subjectivity, which is
even heightened by individuality of language, and, on the other hand, an objective intent—for the aim is an objective description of the company at table,
including the speaker, through a subjective procedure. This procedure leads to a
more meaningful and more concrete illusion of life. Inasmuch as the guest describes a company to which he himself belongs both by inner convictions and

outward circumstances, the viewpoint is transferred to a point within the picture, the picture thus gains in depth, and the light which illuminates it seems to come from within it."

The scene is an artistic triumph of the highest order and marks Petronius, says Auerbach, as a creative genius. Modern novelists, Proust, for example, use exactly the same technique.

A passage in part I of *Gulliver's Travels* leads to similar considerations. Gulliver has established himself in Lilliput; he has captured the enemy fleet, been created a *Nardac*, has extinguished a fire in the royal palace. At the height of his fortunes he receives a secret visit from a friend, a considerable person at court, who comes with a warning of impeachment proceedings already undertaken against him:

"In the several Debates upon this Impeachment, it must be confessed that his Majesty gave many Marks of his great *Lenity*. . . . The Treasurer and Admiral insisted that you should be put to the most painful and ignominious Death. . . . Some of your Servants were to have private Orders to strew a poisonous Juice on your Shirts and Sheets, which would soon make you tear your own Flesh, and die in the utmost Torture. . . .

"*Reldresal* . . . justified the good Thoughts you have of him. He allowed your Crimes to be great; but that . . . if his Majesty, in Consideration of your Services, and pursuant to his own merciful Disposition, would please to spare your Life, and only give order to put out both your Eyes . . . Justice might in some measure be satisfied. . . . [As to the Treasurer's objections to the cost of feeding you, that evil might be provided against, said Reldresal] by gradually lessening your Establishment; by which, for want of sufficient Food, you would grow weak and faint, and lose your Appetite, and consequently decay and consume in a few Months; neither would the Stench of your Carcass be then so dangerous, when it should become more than half diminished; and immediately upon your Death, five or six Thousand of his Majesty's Subjects might, in two or three Days, cut your Flesh from your Bones, take it away by Cart-loads, and bury it in distant Parts to prevent Infection; leaving the Skeleton as a Monument of Admiration to Posterity.

"Thus by the great Friendship of the Secretary [i.e., Reldresal], the whole Affair was compromised."

No warning could be more explicit, and no objective description more convincing. As in the episode from the *Satyricon*, the presentation is entirely subjective. Swift is many removes away: Gulliver as an old man is reporting what he as a much younger man was told by a courtier; the courtier in turn paraphrases or quotes what his Majesty or Skyris Bolgolam or Reldresal said. Even Conrad seldom gets further "inside" an affair than that. We are convinced of the "truth" of the courtier's report precisely because we know he belongs, heart and soul, to what he describes. Friendship may prompt his warning Gulliver, but his rhetoric betrays the identity of his values with those of the persons against whom the warning is given. "Thus by the great Friendship of the Secretary, the whole Affair was compromised." The cool objectivity of the speaker's tone as he details the fate in store for Gulliver is a magnificent commentary on himself and what he represents. The Lilliputian court, like that of Trimalchio, is measured by its own standards.

Petronius allows his scene to carry its own judgment; Encolpius' only comment, when his companion's flow of commentary is interrupted by Trimalchio, is that these have been delightful tales. But Swift adds a further twist or two. It is not enough that the Lilliputian court be damned by the report of one of its own. Gulliver comments:

"Yet, as to myself, I must confess, having never been designed for a Courtier, either by my Birth or Education, I was so ill a Judge of Things, that I could not discover the *Lenity* and Favour of this Sentence; but conceived it (perhaps erroneously) rather to be rigorous than gentle. I sometimes thought of standing my Tryal; for although I could not deny the Facts alledged in the several Articles, yet I hoped they would admit of some Extenuations. But having in my Life perused many State-Tryals, which I ever observed to terminate as the Judges saw fit to direct; I durst not rely on so dangerous a Decision. . . .

"At last I fixed upon a Resolution, for which it is probable I may incur some Censure, and not unjustly; for I confess I owe the preserving mine Eyes, and consequently my Liberty, to my own great Rashness and Want of Experience: Because if I had then known the Nature of Princes and Ministers, which I have since observed in many other Courts, and their Methods of treating Criminals less obnoxious than myself; I should with great Alacrity and Readiness have submitted to so *easy* a Punishment."

The satire spreads like the shock wave from an explosion: from local viciousness to worldwide inhumanity, from the Lilliputian target to the centers of power throughout Europe. Gulliver's bitterness points forward to his later immersion in misanthropy.

Similar as the management of perspective is in the passages from the *Satyricon* and from *Gulliver*, and successful as they both are in achieving the illusion of objective reality, there is still a great difference in their respective tones. The difference is wholly a matter of style. Petronius manages brilliantly to capture the accent and intonation of the speaker himself. The rhythm of the speech, the syntax, the vocabulary—all bespeak the amiable vulgarian who is part of what he describes. Unquestionably here the style is the man. Not so with Swift. His concerns when dealing with human beings are characteristically more abstract.

Oddly, the conversation with the courtier is one of the few in the *Travels* presented as direct quotation; conversations are normally reported in Gulliver's hurried, summarizing way as indirect discourse: I informed him that. . . . I dwellt long upon. . . . I computed. . . . He asked what. . . . He then desired to know. . . . It is as though Swift deliberately avoided the direct confrontation in which individuals would speak with their own voices. But the passage under consideration is in direct discourse: "You are to know, said he, that several Committees of Council have been lately called in the most private Manner on your Account. . . ."; the monologue continues for several pages. Still, we have no real sense that what is said represents a *personal* voice at all. One reason is that the bulk of what the friend reports is something between summary and quotation of what other people have said:

"*Bolgolam*, the Admiral, could not preserve his Temper; but rising up in Fury, said, he wondered how the Secretary durst presume to give his Opinion for preserving the Life of a Traytor: That the Services you had performed, were, by all true Reasons of State, the great Aggravation of your Crimes; that you, who were able to extinguish the Fire, by discharge of Urine in her Majesty's Apartment (which he mentioned with Horror) might, at another time, raise an Inundation by the same Means, to drown the whole Palace."

These are the rhythms that Gulliver as author habitually employs in recording conversation. The speaker is allowed almost no individual tone, as a consequence of which our sense of him as a person is vague. Yet we know unmistakably his relation to certain ideas and moral attitudes. Through him we are shown the motivation of admirals, the "magnanimity" of princes, the objectivity of friends in discussing one's own demise. Insubstantial as he may be, he is an excellent conductor of satire.

But if the characters Gulliver meets on his travels lack individuality, if their voices lack the kind of realism we find in the voice of Encolpius' nameless companion, how different the texture of most of the rest of the work! Swift claims in a letter to Pope that a Bishop in Dublin had read the *Travels* and decided it was full of improbable lies—he hardly believed a word of it; it is as good testimony as any to the extraordinary illusion of verisimilitude Swift imparts to the narrative. "There is an Air of Truth apparent through the whole," says Richard Sympson, the "publisher," attributing it to the circumstantiality of the "plain and simple" style, to which he condescends a little, and of which Gulliver is proud. Gulliver can hardly be conceived of apart from his style; he defines himself by the way he writes, particularly at the beginning:

"My father had a small Estate in *Nottinghamshire*; I was the Third of five Sons. He sent me to *Emanuel-College* in *Cambridge*, at Fourteen Years old, where I resided three Years, and applied my self close to my Studies. . . . I was bound

Apprentice to Mr. *James Bates*, an eminent Surgeon in *London*, with whom I continued four Years. . . . I took Part of a small House in the *Old Jury*; and being advised to alter my Condition, I married Mrs. *Mary Burton*, second Daughter to Mr. *Edmond Burton*, Hosier, in *Newgatestreet*, with whom I received four Hundred Pounds for a Portion."

To define one's life, one enumerates the solid, unproblematic facts that have gone to make it, and one uses solid, unproblematic sentences—simple and straightforward as one's own character.

As the account proceeds the factual texture is thickened:

"By an Observation, we found ourselves in the Latitude of 30 degrees 2 Minutes South. Twelve of our Crew were dead by immoderate Labour, and ill Food; the rest were in a very weak Condition. On the fifth of *November*, which was the beginning of Summer in those Parts, the Weather being very hazy, the Seamen spyed a Rock, within half a Cable's length of the Ship; but the Wind was so strong, that we were driven directly upon it, and immediately split. Six of the crew, of whom I was one, having let down the Boat into the Sea, made a Shift to get clear of the Ship, and the Rock. . . . In about half an Hour the Boat was overset by a sudden Flurry from the North. What became of my Companions in the Boat, as well as of those who escaped on the Rock, or were left in the Vessel, I cannot tell; but conclude they were all lost. For my own Part, I swam as Fortune directed me."

The lack of modulation is striking. The predominantly declarative sentences set out the things that happen in their concrete particularity, piling them up but making no differentiation among them. There is something monstrous in the way that Gulliver can describe the taking of a geographical fix, the deaths of twelve seamen, the wreck of the ship, the loss of his companions, his inability to sit up after his sleep ashore—all in sentences similar in structure and identical in tone. Ordinarily, by his style a writer judges his material, places it for his reader in the context of moral experience. Here, the lack of modulation in the style is a moral commentary on the writer—on Gulliver. Even the King of Brobdingnag is struck by this aspect of Gulliver's style: "He was amazed how so impotent and groveling an Insect as I (these were his Expressions) could entertain such inhuman Ideas, and in so familiar a Manner as to appear wholly unmoved at all the Scenes of Blood and Desolation, which I had painted."

But while we may equate the impassivity of tone with an impassivity of sensibility, we are overwhelmed by the impression of Gulliver's commitment to hard, undeniable fact. Dr. Johnson speaks finely of Swift's "vigilance of minute attention"; we see it most impressively as Gulliver records his reaction to the Lilliputians. The pages are peppered with citations of numbers, figures, dimensions: I count over thirty such citations in the last three paragraphs of chapter 1, each figure increasing our sense of the reality of the scene; for nothing, we tend to think, is so real as number. Gulliver's style approximates an ideal of seventeenth-century scientists: "the marriage of words and things," the deliverance, as Thomas Sprat puts it in a famous passage, of "so many *things*, almost in an equal number of words." Swift (not Gulliver, now) is parodying the life-style that finds its only meaning in things, that lives entirely in the particularity of externals, without being able to discriminate among them. This explains in part the function of the scatological passages of parts I and II which have been found so offensive. The style also helps prepare for the satire on language theory in part III. But, parody or no, Gulliver's style is a marvellous instrument for narration, building easily and with increasing fluidity the substantiality of his world.

Gulliver, then, succeeds in the novelist's great task of creating the illusion of reality. But again we must recall that he is not a novelist. The reality he creates is one of externals only. He does not create a sense of reality about himself—or rather, to step now outside the framework of the *Travels*, Swift does not create a sense of reality about Gulliver. Gulliver is not a character in the sense that Tom Jones, say, is a character. He has the most minimal subjective life; even his passion at the end is hardly rooted in personality. He is, in fact, an abstraction, manipulated in the service of satire. To say this of the principal character of a novel would be damning; but to say it of a work written according to the conventions of Lucian's *A True Story*, the *Satyricon*, *Gargantua* is simply to describe.

The paucity of Gulliver's inner life needs little documentation. To be sure, he is shown as decent and kindly and honorable at the beginning: we are delighted with his stalwart vindication of the honor of the Treasurer's wife, whom malicious gossip accused of having an affair with him. But his life is primarily of the senses. He sees—how superbly he sees!—he hears, smells, feels. Poke him and he twitches; but there is little evidence of rational activity. The *leaping* and *creeping* contest at the Lilliputian court is a diversion for him, nothing more; he sees no resemblance between it and practices in any other court in the world. Except for an occasional (dramatically inconsistent) episode where he is startled into an expression of bitterness, Gulliver's is a life without nuance. The nuances are there, of course, everywhere, but must be supplied by the reader.

In the second voyage Gulliver is even more obviously a mouthpiece for ideas (usually absurd or despicable ideas set up to be subverted by the satire) than a character in his own right. True, he is occasionally reflective: "Undoubtedly Philosophers are in the Right," he muses, as he cowers in fear of being squashed under the foot of the Brobdingnagian, "when they tell us, that nothing is great or little otherwise than by Comparison." And his own thoughts may even reflect satiric insight. On one occasion the King of Brobdingnag remarks on how human (i.e., Brobdingnagian) grandeur can be mimicked by insects like Gulliver. Gulliver is

furious; but the King's mockery works insidiously, and Gulliver begins to wonder
whether he has been injured or not: ". . . if I had then beheld a Company of
English Lords and Ladies in their Finery and Birth-day Cloaths, acting their several Parts in the most courtly Manner of Strutting, and Bowing and Prating; to
say the Truth, I should have been strongly tempted to laugh as much at them as
this King and his Grandees did at me."

Most of the time, however, Gulliver either is impenetrably innocent or embraces the pride and the folly of European civilization with insatiable zeal—all
in the interest of the most mordant satire. We can best see how this works by
looking at the climactic series of dialogues with the King. The scene is projected
with a fine sense of dramatic value: by the King's order Gulliver's box is carried
into the royal closet and set upon the table; Gulliver brings one of his chairs out
of the box, settles himself on a level with the King's head. The two sit there
gravely discussing politics and government and morality. What an opportunity
for Gulliver! "IMAGINE with thy self, courteous Reader, how often I then wished
for the Tongue of *Demosthenes* or *Cicero* that might have enabled me to celebrate the Praise of my own dear native Country in a Style equal to its Merits and
Felicity." As he writes his memoirs, Gulliver reports the substance of the conversations (there were at least seven of them) rather than the conversations themselves:
"I then spoke at large upon the Constitution of an *English* Parliament, partly made
up of an illustrious Body called the House of Peers, Persons of the noblest Blood,
and of the most ancient and ample Patrimonies." The picture he draws of England's history and political institutions is roseate, innocent, abstract—a fat target
for the wickedly acute questions of the King. These (still in indirect discourse)
are at first simple statements in interrogatory form of abuses in the institutions
Gulliver has described: "He asked . . . What Qualifications were necessary in
those who are to be created new Lords: Whether the Humour of the Prince, a
sum of Money to a Court-Lady, or a Prime Minister; or a Design of strengthen-
ing a Party opposite to the publick Interest, ever happened to be Motives in
these Advancements." No indication of the King's own attitude is given (nor
does Gulliver think it either prudent or convenient to repeat his answers) but the
cumulative effect of the long series of queries, all in the same form, is powerful.
As the questions continue to probe into weaknesses both institutional and moral,
the interrogatives become overt accusations: the King was at a loss . . . he wondered to hear . . . he was amazed . . . he laughed at . . . he was perfectly aston-
ished. Under the implacable pounding Gulliver's flimsy structure is reduced to
rubble, and we are prepared for the terrible climax. It gains much effectiveness
by a shift into direct discourse:

"My little Friend *Grildrig*; you have made a most admirable Panegyrick
upon your Country. You have clearly proved that Ignorance, Idleness, and Vice
are the proper Ingredients for qualifying a Legislator. That Laws are best ex-

plained, interpreted, and applied by those whose Interest and Abilities lie in perverting, confounding, and eluding them. I observe among you some Lines of an
Institution, which in its Original might have been tolerable; but these half erased,
and the rest wholly blurred and blotted by Corruptions. It doth not appear from
all you have said, how any one Perfection is required towards the Procurement of
any one Station among you; much less that Men are ennobled on Account of
their Virtue, that Priests are advanced for their Piety or Learning, Soldiers for
their Conduct or Valour, Judges for their Integrity, Senators for the Love of their
Country, or Councellors for their Wisdom. . . . By what I have gathered from
your own Relation, and the Answers I have with much Pains wringed and ex-
torted from you; I cannot but conclude the Bulk of your Natives, to be the most
pernicious Race of little odious Vermin that Nature ever suffered to crawl upon
the Surface of the Earth."

It is a stunning culmination to a scene constructed on the principles of the
formal verse satire. Here the "frame" is provided by the controlling fiction and
given dramatic cogency by all the brilliantly elaborated narrative which has led
up to the encounter. The "I" of the scene—Gulliver—presents the thesis: the
institutions of England are perfection itself; the *adversarius*—the King—demol-
ishes the thesis by his questions and pushes on from institutional criticism to the
shrivelling condemnation of man. The destructive power of his analysis is over-
whelming, but even as he delivers it the "positives" of his world (part B of the
formal verse satire according to Miss Randolph's schematization) are made clear.
Sometimes they appear in the question itself: The King asked, "whether a private
Man's House might not better be defended by himself, his Children, and Family;
than by half a Dozen Rascals picked up at a Venture in the Streets, for small
Wages, who might get an Hundred Times more by cutting their Throats." Sometimes the King makes them explicit: "He said, he knew no Reason, why those
who entertain Opinions prejudicial to the Publick, should be obliged to change,
or should not be obliged to conceal them." In any event the positive and the
negative aspects of the satire confront each other in bold relief; it is rare in Swift
to find the positives of the text in such unequivocal accord with what are manifestly his own positives.

But Swift is not content to leave the scene there. He adds a coda, ham-
mering home the themes and warping Gulliver's character around in the service
of his aim. Gulliver's reaction to the King's judgment of man is an embarrassed
apology; he is sorry that his noble and most beloved country has been subjected
to such treatment, and he is apologetic also about his Majesty:

". . . great Allowances should be given to a King who lives wholly secluded
from the rest of the World, and must therefore be altogether unacquainted with
the Manners and Customs that most prevail in other Nations: The want of
which Knowledge will ever produce many *Prejudices*, and a certain *Narrowness*

of Thinking; from which we and the politer Countries of *Europe* are wholly exempted. And it would be hard indeed, if so remote a Prince's Notions of Virtue and Vice were to be offered as a Standard for all Mankind." (It is not always possible simply to invert Gulliver's statement so as to arrive at Swift's point; witness the fine ambiguity of "it would be hard indeed" in the last sentence.) To ingratiate himself with the King, Gulliver describes (now in indirect discourse but with great graphic power) the destruction wrought by gunpowder and offers him the secret of its manufacture—a secret which would make him "absolute Master of the Lives, the Liberties, and the Fortunes of his People." The King's horror Gulliver can shrug off: "A STRANGE Effect of *narrow Principles* and *short Views*!" From a simple *ingénu*, uncritically bemused by patriotic fervor, Gulliver is made to become an immoralist, advocating doctrines that earlier he has loathed. (In Lilliput he had indignantly refused to be an "Instrument of bringing a free and brave People into Slavery.") Where Gulliver's standards had once represented the satirical positives, here, with the same issue in view, his position is reversed. The satire is consistent, but the characterization is not.

Once again the positives are blocked out with great explicitness. When Gulliver speaks in his own person only the most obvious reversal is required: "The Learning of this People is very defective; consisting only in Morality, History, Poetry and Mathematicks; wherein they must be allowed to excel. But, the last of these is wholly applied to what may be useful in Life; to the Improvement of Agriculture and all mechanical Arts; so that among us it would be little esteemed. And as to Ideas, Entities, Abstractions and Transcendentals, I could never drive the least Conception into their Heads." When Gulliver expounds the King's sentiments, the positives are quite unproblematic: "He confined the Knowledge of governing within very *narrow Bounds*; to common Sense and Reason, to Justice and Lenity, to the speedy Determination of Civil and criminal Causes; with some other obvious Topicks which are not worth considering. And, he gave it for his Opinion; that whoever could make two Ears of Corn, or two Blades of Grass to grow upon a Spot of Ground where only one grew before; would deserve better of Mankind, and do more essential Service to his Country, than the whole Race of Politicians put together." We look in vain for ironic undercutting. Swift might well be speaking in his own voice.

I see no virtue in demonstrating in detail what is universally agreed to: that the third voyage is the weakest of the four. Coleridge called it "a wretched abortion"; and while not everyone shares either the grounds of his dislike or its violence, still one would be hard put to make a case for the uniform literary success of part III. It has, to be sure, its own excellencies. Swift uses satirical techniques here, familiar in his earlier work, that are quite unlike the prevailing methods of the *Travels*. In *A Tale of a Tub* and elsewhere one of his favorite devices is to take literally a metaphorical statement of likeness between two things, then to push the implications of the statement into the grotesque. An ingenious projector in the Academy of Lagado wants to cure the diseases and corruptions of government. He starts with the commonplace notion on which "all Writers and Reasoners have agreed, that there is a strict universal Resemblance between the natural and the political Body." What, then, could be more logical than to treat the peccant humours of a Senate—its tendency to "Spleen, Flatus, Vertigoes and Deliriums—" as one would treat these ailments in individuals? Apothecaries are the answer to good government, and for the body politic there is nothing like a good laxative. If not a laxative, then "Lenitives, Aperitives, Abstersives, Corrosives, Restringents, Palliatives, . . . Cephalalgicks, Ictericks, Apophlegmaticks, Acousticks." The spirit, in this grotesque world, still operates mechanically.

Again, Gulliver's account of eighteenth-century McCarthyism is superb:

"I told him, that in the Kingdom of *Tribnia*, by the Natives called *Langden*, where I had long sojourned, the Bulk of the People consisted wholly of Discoverers, Witnesses, Informers, Accusers, Prosecutors, Evidences, Swearers. . . . It is first agreed and settled among them, what suspected Persons shall be accused of a Plot: Then, effectual Care is taken to secure all their Letters and other Papers, and put the Owners in Chains. These Papers are delivered to a Set of Artists very dextrous in finding out the mysterious Meanings of Words, Syllables and Letters. For Instance, they can decypher a Close-stool to signify a Privy-Council; a Flock of Geese, a Senate; a lame Dog, an Invader; the Plague, a standing Army; a Buzard, a Minister; the Gout, a High Priest; a Gibbet, a Secretary of State; a Chamber pot, a Committee of Grandees; a Sieve, a Court Lady; a Broom, a Revolution; a Mouse-trap, an Employment; a bottomless Pit, the Treasury, a Sink, a C—t; a Cap and Bells, a Favourite; a broken Reed, a Court of Justice; an empty Tun, a General; a running Sore, the Administration."

But clearly this goes beyond McCarthyism. The first target is the interpreters who wrench and distort language for their own infamous purposes; to say that when a man has written the word *gibbet* he intended to signify the Secretary of State is absurd and vicious. Then the satire coils around itself: these grossly unjust distortions of language are, from one point of view, accurate. The Administration *is* a running sore, and its minions are best qualified to make the full identification. Their ingenuity is not yet exhausted: "By transposing the Letters of the Alphabet, in any suspected Paper, they can lay open the deepest Designs of a discontented Party. So for Example, if I should say in a Letter to a Friend, *Our Brother* Tom *hath just got the Piles*; a Man of Skill in this Art would discover how the same Letters which compose that sentence, may be analysed into the following Words; *Resist, a Plot is brought home—The Tour*. And this is the Anagrammatick Method." For benefit of the curious: La Tour was the pseudonym

adopted by Swift's friend Bolingbroke during his exile in France; and the ana-
gram almost works.

Such passages, together with the Juvenalian horror of the Struldbrugg episode, are successful in themselves, but fit into no coherent pattern. Gulliver travels
too much in his third voyage, his experience is too diffuse, and there is a noticeable lapse in the control of materials. One does not have to be inordinately novel-
centered to feel that the haphazard shifts in point of view are confusing and
ineffective. For pages Gulliver can condemn everything he sees on the fantastic
Flying Island, then in the next breath declare it "the most delicious Spot of
Ground in the World." He spins between extreme bitterness and extreme naïveté
as though he had lost a rudder. His gyrations disperse the power of the satire.

Still, the drift of Gulliver's attitude is clearly toward the misanthropic; and
when in the last voyage he finds himself caught between the fixed positions of
the Yahoos and the Houyhnhnms, he is quick to make his unnaturally extreme
choice. There is logic to his change. Like Tennyson's Ulysses, he is part of all that
he has known: he has heard the King of Brobdingnag, he has learned the dirty
secrets of modern history at Glubbdubdrib, he has suffered at the hands of the
most abandoned criminals—those who composed his crew. In a way his misanthropy has been earned. But this is really beside the point; for Gulliver's change
comes about, not in any psychologically plausible way, but because the final,
desperate, internal demands of the satire force him to change.

Part IV of the *Travels* is schematically so like part II that comparison is
inevitable. The intellectual climaxes of the voyages come in conversations between Gulliver and his host of the moment: The King in Brobdingnag, the grey
steed in Houyhnhnm-land. In part II, as we have seen, Swift prepared the scene
carefully, giving it a dramatic setting and structure like that of the formal verse
satire. The conversations in part IV are less sharply dramatized, the climactic
chapters 5 and 6 hardly being set apart from other talks in which Gulliver has
explained to his Master who and what he is. Gulliver discourses on war, law,
commerce, medicine, ministers-of-state, the nobility—the subjects of his rhapsody
in part II—but this time in a flood of vituperation rarely matched in literature.
The Houyhnhnm has little role in this onslaught except to ask an occasional
question. He is as shadowy an interlocutor as some of Juvenal's. The whole tremendous force of these dozen pages is carried by Gulliver's diatribe. For comparison one thinks of Shakespeare's Timon; yet the difference in tone between the two
modes of utterance is enormous. Timon vents personal rage; his hatred comes
boiling forth in a mighty, prolonged curse. Gulliver here expresses no hatred; he
professes simply to be laying before his Master "the whole State of Europe," as
he says. His vein is cold, analytic, impersonal. He speaks of the law:

"I SAID there was a Society of Men among us, bred up from their Youth in the Art of proving by Words multiplied for the Purpose, that *White* is *Black* and *Black* is *White*, according as they are paid. To this Society all the rest of the People are Slaves.

"For Example. If my Neighbor hath a Mind to my *Cow*, he hires a Lawyer to prove that he ought to have my *Cow* from me. I must then hire another to defend my Right; it being against all Rules of *Law* that any Man should be allowed to speak for himself. Now in this Case, I who am the true Owner lie under two great Disadvantages. First, my Lawyer being practiced almost from his Cradle in defending Falshood; is quite out of his Element when he would be an Advocate for Justice, which as an Office unnatural, he always attempts with great Awkwardness, if not with Ill-will. The second Disadvantage is, that my Lawyer must proceed with great Caution: Or else he will be reprimanded by the Judges, and abhorred by his Brethren, as one who would lessen the Practice of the Law. And therefore I have but two Methods to preserve my *Cow*. The first is, to gain over my Adversary's Lawyer with a double Fee; who will then betray his Client, by insinuating that he hath Justice on his Side. The second Way is for my Lawyer to make my Cause appear as unjust as he can; by allowing the *Cow* to belong to my Adversary; and this if it be skilfully done, will certainly bespeak the Favour of the Bench.

"Now, your Honour is to know, that these Judges are Persons . . . picked out from the most dextrous Lawyers who are grown old or lazy: And having been byassed all their Lives against Truth and Equity, lie under . . . a fatal Necessity of favouring Fraud, Perjury and Oppression. . . . It is a Maxim among these Lawyers, that whatever hath been done before, may legally be done again: And therefore they take special Care to record all the Decisions formerly made against common Justice and the general Reason of Mankind. . . . under the Name of *Precedents*."

This goes on for paragraphs.

The two chapters of unimpassioned tirade (one can speak of this style only in terms of paradox) slide imperceptibly between indirect and direct discourse, between the imperfect and the historical present tense, producing sometimes a feeling of dramatic immediacy, sometimes a feeling of rapid survey. As one "fact" is coldly and neatly balanced upon another, there is little modulation in tone, no attempt at climax, no dramatic shift into direct discourse as in part II; it is as though Swift, here at the apogee of Gulliver's progress, scorned such rhetorical tricks, as Gulliver himself claims to do, content to let his "plain Matter of Fact" carry the burden. In its impassive efficiency the style reminds one in some respects of an official Air Force report of a successful bombing raid on a large city.

But this is overstated. The most obvious rhetorical device used here is the exaggeration which pushes Gulliver's account into the realm of the grotesque. We can no more believe in the reality of Gulliver's lawyers than we can believe in Falstaff's tales of his prowess at Gadshill: the two passages have something in common. These lawyers are superhuman, true giants of duplicity. They belong in a far more ideal world than any we know; we can even (unless we are too shocked, or unless we are lawyers) laugh. For obscure reasons, the exaggeration makes our pleasure possible, while it in no way weakens the destructive force of the satiric attack.

Swift uses another favorite stylistic maneuver here—the incongruous catalogue: ". . . vast Numbers of our People are compelled to seek their Livelihood by Begging, Robbing, Stealing, Cheating, Pimping, Forswearing, Flattering, Suborning, Forging, Gaming, Lying, Fawning, Hectoring, Voting, Scribling, Stargazing, Poysoning, Whoring, Canting, Libelling, Free-thinking, and the like Occupations: Every one of which Terms, I was at much Pains to make him understand." It is a noxious enumeration, saved from mere ranting by the incongruity. Syntactical equivalence in a list of this kind obviously implies moral equivalence. Thus stargazing and canting come to equal murder. At first sight the conjunction is amusing (as is the picture of Gulliver spending days in the intricate job of translation); but the final satiric insinuation is that in a sense the equivalence holds: common to all the "Occupations" is a perversion of reason and morality which can lead only to disaster. Precisely this is the burden of the great satire contemporary with *Gulliver's Travels*, Pope's *Dunciad*.

Such rhetorical flourishes are rare in the climactic two chapters of the fourth voyage, however. Their overriding function is to develop with cold implacability the horror of English civilization as Gulliver sees it. Like Timon and like Alceste, Gulliver has assumed the role of satirist, and from this point on he broadens his target to include humanity itself: "When I thought of my Family, my Friends, my Countrymen, or human Race in general, I considered them as they really were, *Yahoos* in Shape and Disposition."

Against the destructiveness of Gulliver's onslaught, we look for the kind of positives that are evident in the episode of the Brobdingnagian King. We naturally turn to the Houyhnhnms who represent to Gulliver (and surely in some sense to Swift) one pole of an antinomy: "The Perfection of Nature" over against the repulsiveness of Yahoo-man. Both Gulliver and the Houyhnhnms are at pains to point out wherein Houyhnhnm perfection lies. It is first physical: Gulliver is lost in awe of the "Strength, Comeliness and Speed" of the horses, whereas he can view his own person only with detestation. The Houyhnhnms themselves are emphatic on the deficiencies of the human physique: Gulliver's hands are too soft to walk on, his nails too short to claw with, his face flat, nose prominent, eyes misplaced, etc. Houyhnhnm perfection is next mental: the horses' lives are "wholly governed" by reason, an infallible faculty, at least to the degree that there is nothing "problematical" about it; reason strikes them with immediate conviction, so that opinion and controversy are unknown. Their perfection is finally moral. They lead austere lives devoted to temperance, industry, and cleanliness; they have no idea of what is evil in a rational creature, have no vice, no lusts, and their passions are firmly controlled by the rational faculty. Their principal virtues are friendship and benevolence, which extend to the whole race; and love as we understand it is unknown. For Gulliver the Houyhnhnms are the repository of all that is good.

Here are positives in abundance, the only question being whether they are unqualifiedly Swift's positives. Most critics have felt that they are and that *Gulliver's Travels* (to say nothing of Swift's character) suffers thereby. Coleridge, for example, writes: ". . . the defect of the work is its inconsistency; the Houyhnhnms are not rational creatures, *i.e.*, creatures of perfect reason; they are not progressive. . . . they, *i.e.*, Swift himself—has a perpetual affectation of being wiser than his Maker . . . and of eradicating what God gave to be subordinated and used; *ex. gr.*, the maternal and paternal affection. . . . In short, critics in general complain of the Yahoos; I complain of the Houyhnhnms." F. R. Leavis writes that the Houyhnhnms "stand for Reason, Truth, and Nature, the Augustan positives, and it was in deadly earnest that Swift appealed to these"—ineffectually appealed, according to Leavis. For G. Wilson Knight, Swift "has none of any *emotional* power" in presenting his positives. "His Hellenic sympathies are all castrated before fit for use. His Utopia is as coldly rational as Milton's Christ." Most recently, Middleton Murry, writing in the same vein, finds the Houyhnhnms "ludicrously inadequate" as symbols of goodness. So, in a carefully qualified sense, they are; and so they were designed to be.

It seems likely that a close reading of Gulliver's fourth voyage is such a shocking experience as to anesthetize the feeling for the ludicrous of even the most sensitive readers (perhaps *particularly* the most sensitive readers). I do not mean to deny the horror of the work, which is radical; but the horror is ringed, as it were, by Swift's mocking laughter. For example, Coleridge is outraged at the way "the horse discourses on the human frame with the grossest prejudices that could possibly be inspired by vanity and self-opinion." Human limbs, Coleridge stoutly insists, are much better suited for climbing and for managing tools than are fetlocks. Swift lacks "reverence for the original frame of man." True, Swift did lack reverence for human clay; but he also wrote the scene of the Houyhnhnm's denigration of the human body as comedy. It is very funny. It is a kind of parody of the eighteenth-century's concern over man's coveting various attributes of the animals, "the strength of bulls, the fur of bears." It is even connected, as we shall see, with the theme of man's coveting supra-human reason. It has the same satirical function as the parallel passage in the second voyage, where the Brobdingnagian philosophers determine after close examination of his form that Gulliver is incapable of preserving his life "either by Swiftness, or climbing of Trees, or digging Holes in the Earth" and must be a *Lusus Naturae* —this kind of determination being "to the unspeakable Advancement of human Knowledge." The equine chauvinism of the Houyhnhnms, amusing as it is, undercuts their authority; it must raise doubts in our minds about their adequacy as guides to *human* excellence, to say nothing of the adequacy of Gulliver, who wants to become a horse and whose capacities in matters requiring moral and intellectual discrimination have not been such as to inspire confidence.

Our dubieties are likely to be strengthened by a careful reading of the last part of the voyage. Although Gulliver presumes to doubt the reasonableness of the Houyhnhnm decision to banish him, he builds his canoe of Yahoo skins and prepares, brokenhearted, to sail into exile. His Master condescends to lift his hoof to Gulliver's mouth; and with this accolade ("Detractors are pleased to think it improbable, that so illustrious a Person should descend to give so great a Mark of Distinction to a Creature so inferior as I") he pushes off in search of an uninhabited island: "so horrible was the Idea I conceived of returning to live in the Society and under the Government of the Yahoos." He reaches an island, where he is the victim of unprovoked attack by savages who wound him with an arrow, and is then picked up, against his will, by Portuguese sailors. An odd situation arises here if we remember that it is the misanthropic Gulliver who is writing his memoirs. It is he who in describing the Portuguese insists on their admirable qualities. The common sailors are "honest"; they address Gulliver with "great Humanity." Captain Pedro de Mendez "was a very courteous and generous Person"; in his dealings with Gulliver he is shown consistently to be a wise and compassionate man. Yet Gulliver is unable to distinguish morally between the savages who had wounded him and this human being whose benevolence is worthy of Houyhnhnm-land. Because the Captain is a man (a Yahoo in Gulliver's terms), Gulliver is perpetually on the verge of fainting at his mere presence; the best he can say of Don Pedro is, "at last I descended to treat him like an Animal which had some little Portion of Reason." Such is the attitude of Gulliver aboard ship. But the Gulliver who is writing (five years, he says, after his return to England) is of precisely the same mind. He shows not the slightest compunction at his earlier fierce denial of spiritual kinship with the Portuguese; he still stuffs his nose against the hated smell of humanity, keeps a long table between his wife and himself, and talks willingly only to horses.

The violence of Gulliver's alienation, his demand (like that of Timon and Alceste) for the absolute, incapacitate him for what Lionel Trilling calls the "common routine" of life—that feeling for the ordinary, the elemental, the enduring which validates all tragic art. Each of Gulliver's voyages begins with a departure from the common routine, each ends with a return to it—to his wife "Mrs. *Mary Burton*, second Daughter to Mr. *Edmond Burton*, Hosier" and their children. This commonplace family represents a fixed point of stability and calm in Gulliver's life, a kind of norm of humble though enduring human values. Gulliver comes from this life, his early literary style is an emblem of it; and it is against the background given by the common routine that his wild rejection shows so startlingly. His first sight of his family after the years of absence produce in him only "Hatred, Disgust, and Contempt. . . . As soon as I entered the House, my Wife took me in her Arms, and kissed me; at which, not having been used to the Touch of that odious Animal for so many Years, I fell in a Swoon for almost an Hour."

In short, Gulliver's *idée fixe* is tested in the world of human experience. The notion that all men are Yahoos cannot accommodate a Don Pedro de Mendez any more than it can accommodate the long-suffering family at Redriff. But this is our own ironic insight, unavailable to Gulliver, who has never been capable of evaluating the significance of his own experience. Gulliver persistently moulds the world according to his idea of it, instead of moulding his idea according to the reality of things—which must include the Portuguese. Such behavior defines comic absurdity as Bergson expounds it. In other contexts this kind of "inversion of common sense" is characteristic of insanity.

The circumstances of Swift's haunted life have been an open invitation to those who would identify him with Gulliver's obsessive and undiscriminating hatred of man—this despite Swift's famous disclaimer: "I have ever hated all nations, professions, and communities," he wrote to Pope, as he was finishing *Gulliver*, "and all my love is toward individuals: for instance, I hate the tribe of lawyers, but I love Counsellor Such-a-one, and Judge Such-a-one: so with physicians—I will not speak of my own trade—soldiers, English, Scotch, French, and the rest. But principally I hate and detest that animal called man, although I heartily love John, Peter, Thomas, and so forth. . . . I have got materials toward a treatise, proving the falsity of that definition *animal rationale*, and to show it would be only *rationis capax*. Upon this great foundation of misanthropy, though not in Timon's manner, the whole building of my Travels is erected."

Gulliver's hatred *is* in Timon's manner, for John, Peter, and Thomas are precisely as odious to him as the worst Yahoo alive. So far removed is he from Swift.

The last words of Gulliver's memoir are part of the complex process of discrediting his vision of the world. He ends with a virulent diatribe against pride, a sin of which he himself is conspicuously guilty. Like the Poet in *Timon*, he whips his own faults in other men. We recall his absurd condescension to Don Pedro: ". . . at last I descend to treat him like an Animal which had some little

Portion of Reason"; his reluctance to exchange the Yahoo skins he wears for Don Pedro's shirts, lest he be defiled. Other manifestations of his pride are charmingly ingenuous. In the last chapter he writes: "I AM not a little pleased that this Work of mine can possibly meet with no Censurers. . . . I write for the noblest End, to inform and instruct Mankind, over whom I may, without Breach of Modesty, pretend to some Superiority. . . . I hope, I may with Justice pronounce myself an Author perfectly blameless." We smile at the vision of Gulliver trotting around like a horse, proclaiming his superiority in a whinny.

But Gulliver's pride has more important implications. His is the pride of reason, the belief that man can and should conduct his life entirely in accord with reason, as do the Houyhnhnms. Reason for them, it will be recalled, is not the faculty of ratiocination, but an innate power: "Neither is *Reason* among them a Point problematical as with us, where Men can argue with Plausibility on both Sides of a Question; but strikes you with immediate Conviction; as it must needs do where it is not mingled, obscured, or discoloured by Passion and Interest." The faculty is unmistakably supra-human. Swift makes the point explicit when he has Gulliver condescend to Don Pedro's "very good *human* Understanding." The italics are Swift's. Houyhnhnm reason reminds one of the faculty innate in the gods of Stoic theology, as they are described in Cicero's *De natura deorum*. Above the vegetable kingdom, above the animals, above man, says the Stoic speaker, is another level of existence: "But the fourth and highest grade is that of beings born by nature good and wise, and endowed from the outset with the innate attributes of right reason and consistency; this must be held to be above the level of man." Houyhnhnm reason is very close to this—close, that is, to the attributes of the gods: far from those of man. In aspiring to this reason, Gulliver is like the philosopher in *The Mechanical Operation of the Spirit* who, his eyes fixed on the stars, allowed his lower parts to be seduced into the ditch. Swift's intense moral realism prompted him always to work for the attainable.

Again, although the Houyhnhnms have emotions and are said to have passions, their emotional life is firmly controlled by reason: their "grand Maxim is, to cultivate Reason, and to be wholly governed by it." We have no impression that the horses must struggle, as men have struggled, to achieve this state of affairs. Compare Stoic doctrine: "Wipe out imagination," wrote Marcus Aurelius, "check impulse: quench desire: keep the governing self [Reason] in its own power." Stoic exaltation of the reason at the expense of the passions represented to many eighteenth-century writers a particularly virulent form of pride. It was a denial of man's nature, of his middle state—that state explored so fully in spatial terms in the first two voyages of *Gulliver*. It was man's effort to rise above himself in the scale of created things. "To be a *Stoic*," wrote Sir William Temple, ". . . one must be perhaps something more or less than a man. . . ." To try to live by reason alone was, as Lovejoy puts it, "an attempt to be unnaturally good and immoderately virtuous." We have "too much weakness for the Stoic's pride," wrote Pope; and a good deal of the *Essay on Man* is devoted to showing the constitutive role of the passions in the nature of man. By advocating for humanity a reason explicitly supra-human, Gulliver exemplifies well the folly of Stoic pride. His moral overstrain is symbolized in his galloping gait and his whinnying tone; his pride is presented dramatically, as, scorning the good about him, he compounds for the shadow of a shadow: two horses and the smell of a stable.

Gulliver, in trying to be a Houyhnhnm, violates the great principle of order:

> In Pride, in reas'ning Pride, our error lies;
> All quit their sphere, and rush into the skies.
> Pride still is aiming at the blest abodes,
> Men would be Angels, Angels would be Gods.
> · · · · · · · · · · · ·
> All this dread ORDER break—for whom? for thee?
> Vile worm!—oh Madness, Pride, Impiety!

Pope's tone is fervent, for the passages adumbrate catastrophe. Gulliver's venture into the same madness leads not to cosmic disaster but to the ridiculous.

"Oh! if the world had but a dozen Arbuthnots in it, I would burn my Travels," Swift wrote to Pope in the letter cited above. Middleton Murry suggests plausibly that Swift had Arbuthnot in mind as a model for Don Pedro de Mendez; in any event, the two men, one in life and one in fiction, redeem mankind from the charge of total Yahooism. In the character of Don Pedro—slender reed!—Swift makes the strongest statement of his positives in this final part of the *Travels*. To be sure, the destructive criticism—the satire—often carries its own implied standard of excellence. It seems folly to expect a satirist who attacks war to say overtly that he favors peace. But Swift makes a further gesture. Insofar as Gulliver's positives are defined by the *exigence d'absolu* represented by the Houyhnhnms, they are largely discredited as unavailable to man; but by a neat ironic twist Swift has Gulliver, in the Letter to Captain Sympson, voice standards more or less viable in human terms. It is a feature of Gulliver's absurdity that he thinks seven months ample time for Yahoos to have been reformed by his book. Yet,

"I cannot learn that my Book hath produced one single Effect according to my Intentions: I desired you would let me know by a Letter, when Party and Faction were extinguished; Judges learned and upright; Pleaders honest and modest, with some Tincture of common Sense; and *Smithfield* blazing with Pyramids of Law-Books; the young Nobility's Education entirely changed; the Physicians banished; the Female *Yahoos* abounding in Virtue, Honour, Truth, and good Sense: Courts and Levees of great Ministers thoroughly weeded and swept; Wit, Merit and Learning rewarded; all Disgracers of the Press in Prose and Verse, condemned to eat nothing but their own Cotten, and quench their Thirst with their own Ink. These, and a Thousand other Reformations, I firmly counted upon by your Encouragement; as indeed they were plainly deducible from the Precepts delivered in my Book."

The normative urgency in Swift rarely finds distinguished utterance, and the positives here are perfunctorily stated. Doubtless they are as unattainable in a literal sense as those of the Houyhnhnms, but one does not have to neigh to utter them.

As to the satirists in the work: The King of Brobdingnag functions as one, we know, in the scene we have discussed and again when he takes Gulliver up in his right hand, strokes him, laughs, and asks whether Gulliver is Whig or Tory. It is a splendid passage, reducing in a gesture the folly of party faction to the level of High-Heels versus Low-Heels in Lilliput. The King speaks from standards indistinguishable from those of Swift; and the Brobdingnagian "mixed" government probably represents Swift's notion of an ideal not entirely beyond man's capacity to achieve. The rarefied atmosphere of Houyhnhnm-land could hardly support satire, although Gulliver once accuses his Master of a "malicious Insinuation, which debased human Understanding below the Sagacity of a common *Hound*"; but the satirist of part IV is not a horse, it is Gulliver. Occasionally he displays a satirical technique of great sophistication, as when he wishes that a number of Houyhnhnms could be sent to Europe to teach "the first Principles of Honour, Justice, Truth, Temperance, publick Spirit, Fortitude, Chastity, Friendship, Benevolence, and Fidelity. The *Names* of all which Virtues are still retained among us in most Languages, and are to be met with in modern as well as ancient Authors; which I am able to assert from my own small Reading."

But this is rare. Gulliver's function is to lay bare the rottenness at the core of human institutions and to show man what, in Gulliver's view, he is: an animal cursed with enough reason to make him more repulsive and more dangerous than the Yahoos. Satirists have always used the transforming power of language to reduce man to the level of the beast, but few have debased man as systematically and as ruthlessly as does Gulliver. To find parallels one must go to the theologians. John Donne describes man's mortal condition in one of his Lincoln Inn sermons: "Between that excremental jelly that thy body is made of at first, and that jelly which thy body dissolves to at last; there is not so noisome, so putrid a thing in nature." "What is man," asks Jeremie Taylor, "but a vessel of dung, a stink of corruption, and, by birth, a slave of the devil?" It may be, as Mr. Roland Frye contends, that Swift's image of the Yahoo was adapted from the vast body of Christian symbolism which emphasizes the loathsome degradation of man's state. It would be possible in that case to think of Gulliver as a satirist of man within the Christian tradition. But *Swift*, as this essay has tried to show, writes as a humanist, not as a theologian. *His* satire undercuts Gulliver's vision of man, which is shown dramatically, concretely, to be incommensurate with man's total experience. The vision, to be sure, has a certain abstract cogency, and in Houyhnhnm-land it carries conviction; but Gulliver (like Timon and Alceste) fails to assume the human burden of discriminating morally between man in the abstract and John, Peter, Thomas, and Don Pedro de Mendez. Swift, in life and in this work, insists upon that responsibility.

This reading of *Gulliver's Travels* dissolves a logical paradox. Insofar as Gulliver's vision of man obtains, Swift is implicated: if all men are Yahoos, the creator of Gulliver is a Yahoo among the rest, and *Gulliver's Travels* (and all literary works whatsoever) are no more than the noisome braying of an odious beast. As a clergyman, there is a sense in which Swift might have accepted those implications; but as a humanist and an author he could not. He could accept his own involvement in the great range of human folly which Gulliver avidly depicts, but he could not accept the total Yahoodom of man.

RONALD PAULSON

The Parody of Eccentricity

And, Oh, it can no more be questioned,
That beauties best, proportion, is dead.
　　　　—DONNE, "First Anniversary"

I. THE CHARACTERISTIC TONE

Swift's *Tale of a Tub* is one of the "eccentric" books of English literature. From
it the mind moves naturally back to the anatomies of Rabelais and Montaigne in
France or of Nashe, Burton, Browne, and Urquhart of Cromarty in England.
Such phenomena, it can be argued, are best left alone by Reason with his "Tools
for cutting, and opening, and mangling, and piercing." The result of analysis
may be to exorcise the characteristic tone, or at least the one for which the book
is famous; when all puzzles are solved the book, being no longer a puzzle, is no
longer the same.

My justification for analyzing the *Tale of a Tub* lies in the evident need for
a close reading, which Swift himself made a gesture toward sanctioning when he
wrote his "Author's Apology" to meet the accusations of irreligion that were
promptly leveled at his book. Over and over through the years since its publication, and largely because of its form, the *Tale of a Tub* has been accused of being
(1) an outright attack on religion, (2) an expression of disorder, which is nihilis-
tic, or (3) an elaborate joke which disregards overall unity for the hilarity of
momentary incongruities.

Most Swift criticism before the twentieth century deals with the *Tale*'s supposed religious deficiencies. It is on religious grounds that its first (rather preju-
diced) critics, Wotton, Dennis, and Blackmore, attack it. Dr. Johnson agrees that
it is "certainly a dangerous example," and Scott, De Quincey, Thackeray, and

From *Theme and Structure in Swift's "Tale of a Tub."* © 1960 by Yale University Press.

other nineteenth-century critics generally follow this line. All of them manage to steer clear of an actual examination of the text, perhaps because they do not expect to find order beneath the surface of disorder; such a discovery would disturb the characteristic tone. The idea of the disrespectful theme is such a strong preconception that the critics who see admirable qualities in the *Tale* either talk about Swift the man as a damned titan, or, like Hazlitt, they praise its style, calling it "one of the most masterly compositions in the language, whether for thought, wit, or style," but altogether ignore the problem of what the "thought" may be. Scott, while praising the brilliance of expression, admits that it "was considered [by contemporaries], not unreasonably, as too light for a subject of such grave importance," and "in some parts of the *Tale*" Swift's wit has "carried him much beyond the bounds of propriety."

In our own day John Middleton Murry has continued the tradition of religious criticism: "This cannot be merely a careless fling that strikes St. Paul by accident," he says. "Swift must have aimed it." And for William Empson the *Tale* is a reduction of Christian terminology and imagery to their grossest physical equivalents. F. R. Leavis believes that the *Tale*'s ironic intensity is purely destructive, and that it is "essentially a matter of surprise and negation; its function is to defeat habit, to intimidate and to demoralize." A well-meaning critic like Henry Craik has tried to dispel the religious bugaboo by pointing out that only one-third of the text pertains to religion, while two-thirds is devoted to the abuses of learning. But he settles for a harmless book at the expense of unity, for he admits that these two elements divide the work. George Sherburn implies that in the *Tale* Swift is sometimes "not clear as to just what he wants to do, and allows himself a virtuosity of witty effervescence that delights or wounds by turns." Criticism thus runs the gamut from seeing the *Tale* as consciously irreligious to seeing it as lacking a positive philosophy, and finally to seeing it as uncertain of intention. Murry, for example, finds it "primarily a manifestation of the comic spirit"—it is not possible to take it seriously, except at our peril. Even Herbert Davis, who has noted Swift's employment of literary parody, tends to take the *Tale* as a *jeu d'esprit*, impatient of too much analysis; while Leavis thinks that "this savage exhibition is mainly a game, played because it is the insolent pleasure of the author."

We can conclude that closely allied to this preconception of the characteristic tone and the disrespectful theme is the belief that satirists like Swift did not seek unity or consistency in their works; that Swift in his major works was the same sort of journalist he was in his *Examiners* and party pamphlets. All apparent inconsistencies can thus be explained as either the satirist's roving fire or Swift's playfulness.

More recent critics have devoted themselves to seeking consistency and unity in Swift's works—more successfully with *Gulliver's Travels*, however, than with the *Tale*. The rhetorical critics of the last few years have cleared up such crucial misunderstandings as the relationship between Swift and the speaker of the *Tale*, but they tend to slight the religious question, demonstrating instead the brilliance of Swift's persuasion.

It is my contention that one must try to come to terms with the *Tale* and determine what its particular kind of unity is, assuming that a work of art (in order to be one) must be in some way unified. There are, of course, different kinds of unity, for each work of art, as it creates its own world, has its own laws and logic. The question of whether Swift consciously sought unity in his works can best be answered by remembering that Swift, Pope, and their group were conscious inheritors of the Renaissance-Christian ideals, an important one being the ideal of unity and harmony of proportion.

To cope with Swift's *Tale of a Tub* the critic can neither ignore technical considerations of structure and satiric method nor reason away the religious accusations. The defender of Swift must accept the fact that, whatever statistics can be produced to the contrary, the religious theme is the crucial one to an understanding of the *Tale*. A misunderstanding which lies at the bottom of the accusation of irreligion is brought to light in a comment of Scott's. He refers to the *Tale*'s being "recommended by Voltaire to his proselytes, because the ludicrous combinations which are formed in the mind of the peruser, tend to lower the respect due to revelation." Such juxtapositions appear to be disrespectful when aimed at revelation. The misunderstanding implicit here is between two views of religion and two views of man. One of these sees "ludicrous combinations" as destroying man's dignity, while the other sees them as holding him down to his natural size. These two views are irreconcilable as to man's relation to God and, accordingly, as to the nature of revelation. Our look at the *Tale of a Tub* will demonstrate why they are irreconcilable and why and how Swift accepts the less optimistic of the two views.

Because its theme is so closely connected with its form, we shall approach the *Tale* through the eccentricity we noted at the beginning of this section, the oddness which has both fascinated and repelled Swift's readers.

II. CHARACTERISTICS OF SEVENTEENTH-CENTURY FORM: A POSSIBLE INTERPRETATION

We shall begin our inquiry by seeking a distinction between Swift's *Tale of a Tub* and the other anatomies whose eccentricity brought them to mind; and so for our purpose we must look on these works less with the reverence due historically important objects than with an inquiring eye to the elements that make them eccentric and similar to the *Tale*.

Seen in this way, the anatomies of Nashe, Burton, and Browne are at once compost heaps of information and charming personal documents; and the list I have suggested could be extended to include sermons and various other forms which show the same characteristics, though on a smaller scale. The sermon of a Donne or an Andrewes is as exhaustive and personal on its given topic as is Burton on his. The divine means to demonstrate the truth of his interpretation of Scripture by showing every bit of evidence pointing to it, from the enumeration of authorities to the exploitation of syntax and semantics. Burton, on the other hand, collects all the information he can find about theories of the physiological causes of melancholy, but his object is to show the disagreements and incongruities among these theories in order to suggest the probability of psychological causes. Burton and the divine have in common the desire to prove something beyond the shadow of a doubt.

In the same way the anatomies of Montaigne and Browne are similar in structure but aim at precisely opposite conclusions. Montaigne produces fact after fact, customs that conflict, beliefs that do not agree, creating a great monument to the inconsistency and stubbornness of the human mind and a triumphant proof that reason is inadequate, from which proof he concludes, "O what a soft and easy and wholesome pillow is ignorance and freedom from care to rest a well-screwed-on headpiece!" Since reason is unreliable, one should examine the evidence but withhold judgment. Browne accumulates his evidence, not unlike Montaigne's; but having destroyed superstitions and having proved that a reasonable man cannot possibly believe in, for example, immortality, he concludes (with an 'O Altitudo!") that this is all the more reason for one to do so.

In each of these cases, however, the conclusion is all but submerged in the evidence, which, one feels, exists as much for its own sake as for that of the argument. What makes these writers still interesting after three hundred years is, in fact, the mass of detail with which they clutter their search for an absolute. But seeking to establish universals, they demonstrate a stronger probability of nominalism, and their conflict between the validity of faith and the validity of reason ends with the incidentals collapsing the main argument.

The Rabelaisian anatomy too is nominalist in method, collecting all manner of stories, jokes, poems, songs, all the paraphernalia of the medieval popular sermon. But, as Erich Auerbach has pointed out, "Rabelais' entire effort is directed toward playing with things and with the multiplicity of their possible aspects; upon tempting the reader out of his customary and definite way of regarding things, by showing him phenomena in utter confusion; upon tempting him out into the great ocean of the world, in which he can swim freely, though it be at his own peril." Every page, by presenting the madness and inconsistency of men, bespeaks freedom of choice and invites the reader to give way to the natural man in him. The question of Rabelais' relation to Christian dogma is not important in the overall effect of his work; rather the "imitation" of chaos is itself something at which the church tends to look askance, particularly when it appears to be urged upon the reader as a way of life. This is a far cry from the intention of either Montaigne or Browne—but it is a conclusion the reader may draw from them too if he is so inclined.

The first characteristic of these works, then, is an encyclopedic fullness in a protean disorder. The second is the personal quality. Rabelais is portraying the individual, free of restraint; and there is an equally striking autonomy in Montaigne's aloof and uncommitted "que sais-je?" Montaigne intends, by showing that man's only basis for certainty is his own subjective opinion, to prove man's inadequacy and need for the authority of tradition or common forms; but this emphasis is very easily shifted to an exaltation of the individual's subjective opinion. An underlying assumption in seventeenth-century literature that must not be discounted is the ever-growing interest in self, derived in part from Renaissance humanism and in part from the trend toward subjectivity manifested in all branches of the Protestant Reformation. At its logical extreme, this was the belief that everything one writes is interesting because it is self-expression. Although the seventeenth-century trend toward self-expression was only a whisper compared to what would come in the nineteenth century, it is safe to say that Montaigne was read as much for the revelation of an interesting mind as for his pyrrhonist epistemology.

In order to see how subjectivity was reflected in style and form we can begin with a passage from John Donne, who, speaking of the Metaphysical style of preaching, explains that

> the Holy Ghost in penning the Scriptures delights himself, not only with a propriety, but with a delicacy, and harmony, and melody of language; with height of Metaphors, and other figures, which may work great impressions upon the Readers, and not with barbarous, or triviall, or market or homely language . . . and they mistake it much that thinke, that the Holy Ghost hath rather chosen a low, and barbarous, and homely style, then an eloquent, and powerful manner of expressing himselfe.
>
> (Sermon 55, "Preached at St. Paul's upon Christmas day, 1626")

Donne's God is unashamedly in his own image: to be God—or the Holy Ghost —is to be grandiose and copiously creative, almost Rabelaisian. In the passage cited he piles "delicacy" upon "propriety," and "harmony" and "melody" upon these—suggesting a great abundance rather than any order or decorum an earlier generation might have associated with God. Donne's syntax is, in fact, disordered, and each new adjective tries to go the last one better.

To see the norm from which a style like Donne's deviates one need only turn back a few years to the writing of Richard Hooker:

> The light would never be so acceptable, were it not for that usual intercourse of darkness. Too much honey doth turn to gall; and too much joy even spiritually would make us wantons. Happier a great deal is that man's case, whose soul by inward desolation is humbled, than he whose heart is through abundance of spiritual delight lifted up and exalted above measure. Better it is sometimes to go down into the pit with him, who, beholding darkness and bewailing the loss of inward joy and consolation, crieth from the bottom of the lowest hell, "My God, my God, why hast thou forsaken me?" than continually to walk arm in arm with angels, to sit as it were in Abraham's bosom, and to have no thought, no cogitation, but "I thank my God it is not with me as it is with other men." No, God will have them that shall walk in light to feel now and then what it is to sit in the shadow of death. A grieved spirit therefore is no argument of a faithless mind.

This passage from Hooker's sermon "Of the Certainty and Perpetuity of Faith in the Elect" shows, in the control exerted by the periodic sentence, the employment of an external order. The first and second sentences, with their antitheses and point, could have been written by Donne or Andrewes. But the third sentence and then the fourth, pivoting on "Happier" and "Better . . . than," fill in their skeletons with clauses and phrases conveying information, each in an orderly relation to the central antithesis of the sentence. In the Ciceronian period the dependent members are arranged in climactic order, each directing the reader toward the principal member which, suspended until the end, acts as capstone to an almost architectural structure. The same can be said of the overall form of Hooker's sermons or of the *Laws of Ecclesiastical Policy*. Every proof has its place in the argument, which moves forward like an army in review. The result is a "fixed" quality, a finality and forethought which are not apparent in Donne.

In the loose (or anti-Ciceronian) style the function of the sentence as a sorter and arranger of information is lost. Its function is rather, as Morris Croll has written, "to express individual variances of experience in contrast with the general and communal ideas which the open design of oratorical style is so well adapted to contain." The writer's individuality will not be fettered by the Ciceronian forms. "I shall here write down my thoughts without arranging them," wrote Pascal, "but not perhaps in deliberate disorder; that is the proper order, and it will convey my intention by its very want of order." The sentence becomes a medium for showing the mind moving toward truth, rather than for presenting truth, and accordingly becomes so flexible as to be almost coextensive with the author's thought, in subtlety and duration. The larger structure of the work becomes similarly fluid, its most patent sign of freedom being the digression, its logical end the pile of notes that Pascal left behind him. There is no ordering from without; the sentences, paragraphs, and chapters record the thoughts the way—and in the order—they were thought.

The aesthetic which explains the trend we have been examining is summed up in Bacon's words: "There is no excellent beauty that hath not some strangeness in the proportion." Its literary guides were the poets of the Roman Silver Age and their calculated disorder, instead of the ordered sanity of the Golden Age. Art historians call the period mannerist, and in Wylie Sypher's study, *Four Stages of Renaissance Style*, it is said to be characterized by "no logical focus for the composition," "no release; only tension," or by "techniques of disproportion and disturbed balance . . . with oblique or mobile points of view and strange— even abnormal—perspectives that yield approximations rather than certainties."

There is, however, more than one reason for aiming at the eccentric or unique: we have noticed its use as a presentation of the individual seeking self-knowledge; but it can also be a presentation of the self to catch attention, or it can become merely a device for moving an audience.

In our survey of seventeenth-century literature let us, for simplicity's sake, confine ourselves to the three areas Swift singles out for attention in the three "oratorial machines": the pulpit, the gallows, and the stage itinerant. Beginning with the pulpit, we can observe that in the seventeenth century both Puritan and Anglican preachers exploited the opportunities for brilliance inherent in a loose syntax, in vivid metaphors, and in the sudden outburst of rhetorical passion. What followed was the great age of pulpit eloquence, when people crowded to hear their favorite preachers. It is possible to infer from this fact alone that expression became at least as important to congregations as the doctrine expressed. For example, schemata are used by Hooker as traditional patterns of expression —*parison, isocolon, homoioteleuton*—which organize and hold together the periodic structure of his sentences. In Andrewes' sermons there is a tendency— which becomes flagrant in his less scrupulous imitators—to use schemata for sheer word play; their contribution to the overall structure is minimal. To take a well-known example, here is a passage from Andrewes' ninth Nativity Sermon:

> For, if this Childe by *Immanuel*, GOD *with us*; then without this
> Childe, this *Immanuel*, we be without GOD. *Without Him, in this
> World* (saith the *Apostle*;) And, if without him, in this, without Him,
> in the next: And, if without Him there, if it be not *Immanu-el*, it
> will be *Immanu-hel*; and that, and no other place, will fall (I feare

me) to our share. Without Him, this we are: What, with Him? Why,
if we have Him; and GOD, by Him; we need no more: *Immanu-el*
and *Immanu-all*. All that we can desire is, for us to be *with Him*,
with GOD; and He to be *with us*. And we, from Him, or He from
us, never to be parted.

These members, for all the connected word play, give the impression of being
exploratory. The object is to present the process of learning, or the process of
Biblical exegesis, rather than the accomplished fact. The schemata have the effect
of drawing attention to a point being made, or of awakening the congregation to
a point about to be made; but when used to excess, they direct attention to the
preacher himself. Accordingly, among the young and ambitious preachers the best
way to attract attention was by employing the most extravagant, eye-catching wit.

A chief criticism leveled at this style by the reformers of the Restoration
was that "the general sense of the [Biblical] text was totally neglected, while
every single word of it was separately considered under all its possible meanings."
One of the wittiest of these reformers, John Eachard, makes up an amusing example of the Metaphysical emphasis on individual words. Using the text, "But
his delight is in the Law of the Lord," the preacher begins "BUT, *This* BUT . . . *is
full of spiritual wine; we will broach it, and taste a little, then proceed.*" Eachard
adds that he would have been happier if the preacher had "spoken in *Latin*; and
told us, that this *sed* or *verum, enim, vero*, is full of *spiritual wine*; For then the
wit would have been more admired for lying a great way off." But if the Angli-
cans sometimes put too much emphasis on a word, the Puritans were "much in
love with new-minted Words, in which they thought there were great Mysteries
concealed." While the Metaphysicals use learned words, Latin and Greek citations, and schemata, "so neither can the [Puritans'] whimsical Cant of *Issues,
Products, Tendencies, Breathings, In-dwellings, Rollings, Recumbencies*, and
Scriptures misapplied, be accounted Divinity."

Another eye-catcher is metaphor, whose vividness depends largely upon
the juxtaposition of a physical, sensory object with a spiritual concept, as in
Andrewes' comparison of the Gunpowder Plot to the conception of a child:
"there is not onely *fructus ventris*, there is *partus mentis*: the *minde conceives*,
as well as the *wombe*: the word [conceiving] is like proper, to both. Men have
their *wombe*, but it lieth higher, in them; as high as their *hearts*; and that which
is there *conceived*, and *bred*, is a *birth*." The "Gunpowder sermons" contain
Andrewes' most extravagant wit; here we find such phrases as "Through the
Cisterne and Conduit of all *Thy mercies, Iesus Christ*." But this need only be
compared with a metaphorical passage unfolded by a Puritan: "Christ can come
by you suddenly in a blast of a whirlwind, in a preaching, and cast in a coal at the
window of your soul, and leave it smoking, and slip His way. And He can shoot

an arrow of love even to the feathers, and post away Himself, and say, 'Pack you out. Here is a bone for you to gnaw on.' " Samuel Rutherford, the Scotch Presbyterian who wrote this, also advises "Thank God for the smell of Christ when ye cannot get Himself." Joseph Glanvill noticed that Puritan preachers "tell the people that they must roll upon *Christ*, close with *Christ*, get into *Christ*, get a saving interest in the Lord *Christ*." While the Puritans avoided the literary and the learned, the everyday images to which they resorted brought religion down either to the concrete level of wrestling matches and "a busie Trade," or to the vagueness of "get into *Christ*." What Andrewes' and the Puritans' sermons have in common is the use of the unexpected, of the momentary surprise.

Another characteristic of the seventeenth-century sermon is a tendency to allow one of these momentary surprises to grow, replacing more conventional structures with the logic of a metaphor. The speaker, once committed to his vehicle, begins to create meaning which may not be at every point consonant with his intention. "The more I think of it," says Andrewes, concerning the comparison of the Gunpowder Plot to parturition, "the more points of correspondence do offer themselves to me."

> 1. The *vessels* first give forth themselves, as so many *embrio's*: 2. The *vault*, as the *wombe*, wherein they lay so long: 3. They that conceived this device were the *mothers*, cleare: 4. the *fathers*, were the *fathers* (as they delight to be called) though, oft, little more than boyes; but here, *right fathers*, in that they perswaded, it might be, why not? might be *lawful*; nay *meritorious*, then: so, it was they, that did animate, gave a *soule* (as it were) to the *treason*. 5. The *conception* was, when the *powder*, as the *seed* was conveighed in: 6. The *articulation*, the touching of them, in order, just as they should stand: 7. the *covering* of them, with *wood* and *fagots*, as the drawing a *skin*, over them: 8. The *Venerunt ad partum*, when all was now ready, *traine* and all: 9. The *Mid-wife*, he that was found with the *match* about him, for the purpose: 10. And *partus*, the *birth* should have bin upon the giving *fire*. If the *fire* had come to the *powder*, the *children had come to the birth*.

As the Royal Society and modern semanticists have complained, a metaphor changes the thing itself, while the auricular figures employed by Hooker and the Elizabethans in general merely underline meaning.

Sound itself often became divorced from meaning in this century of the sermon. There is evidence that the Anglican congregations liked to hear the sound of the Greek and Latin quotations in sermons when they were altogether unintelligible to them. In 1668 Robert South, commenting on the problem in a sermon at Christ Church, Oxford, recognizes a sort of sensory appeal in the "fustian

bombast" of these preachers, because "none are so transported and pleased with
it as those who least understand it." He points out that "the greatest admirers of
it are the grossest, the most ignorant, and illiterate country people, who, of all
men, are the fondest of highflown metaphors and allegories, attended and set off
with scraps of Greek and Latin." The sensory element can be found in the Puritan preacher's coughs and hems; it appears to be a fact that dissenter preachers
"looked upon coughing and hemming as ornaments of speech" to such an extent
that they included them in the printed texts of their sermons. Finally, there were,
among the Puritans, "those strange new Postures used by some in the Delivery of
the Word"—"Such as shutting the eyes, distorting the face, and speaking through
the nose," which South noticed. These sounds and motions have, of course, the
two explanations we noticed earlier: they reveal the speaker's mind, and they can
move an audience. For example, the visual gymnastics of dissenter preachers may
convey the mind's agitation and suggest the inexpressible it is moving toward.

What we have said of the pulpit can be said of the second oratorial machine
as well. The gallows, "the symbol of faction," represents the polemical writings
dealing with church and state. It is, of course, always characteristic of a polemic
to persuade at whatever cost to logic or consistency; but particularly so in the
century that saw writers like William Prynne, whose pamphlets are simply a mad
extension of the anatomies produced by Burton and Browne: "a torrent of un-
sorted, unconsidered precedents and citations. If one did not fit, another might."
Prynne's prestige, which gave authority to his most random erudition, depended
largely on the figure of "Prynne the martyr" which accompanied, and played so
large a part in, all of his pamphlets. The influence of Foxe's martyrology led not
only to the spiritual autobiographies of Puritan sermons but also to the authority
of martyrdom in the accounts of men like Burton, Lilburne, or Prynne in the
pillory. Offering a possible source for Swift's pulpit which "exerts a strong influence on ears," Henry Burton (then earless) wrote that the pillory "was the hap-
piest pulpett hee had ever preacht in." Both Burton and Lilburne called the day
of their martyrdom their wedding day, and capitalized upon it as an exemplum
or *type* of the persecuted saint or the crucified Christ. The individual's experience
has thus become an irrefutable piece of logic in the Puritan polemic; personality
has replaced argument.

A more respectable example, however, is John Milton, who by Swift's time
had become a great Whig-Dissenter prophet. Even Milton takes time off in the
middle of his *Reason of Church Government* to insert a long autobiographical
digression (as preface to the second part), and the *Apology for Smectymnuus* is essentially the continuation of this self-portrait. Although the *Apology* is strikingly
digressive (a formal eulogy of the Long Parliament is inserted at one place between point-for-point confutations of Bishop Hall), the level of the sentence is

perhaps most instructive as a gauge of Milton's form. The general tone of the syntax is consonant with the role Milton gives himself in the autobiographical parts: that of a prophet or seer, which requires rolling cadences and resounding periods. But this syntax, while often giving the impression of being Ciceronian, collapses into anacoluthon or rambles off into matters that are unrelated to the subject of the sentence. The frequent confusion of Milton's syntax is the result not simply of overloading a subordinated structure, but rather of the subordinated matter's being not really subordinated as it would appear to be; its grammatical links are belied by the erratic order of the thought. In other words, we have here the employment of an ostensibly Ciceronian style without the periodic turn of mind so important in the prose of a writer like Hooker. While Milton's periodic opening suggests a kind of order and certainty, of the sort he is evoking in Presbyterianism, the rest of the sentence demonstrates a freedom that is associated with the anti-Ciceronian style; and, as in the case of Prynne, reliance is placed on sheer effect.

In the branches of literature that are covered by the stage itinerant (plays and Grub Street productions) the emphasis on sheer effect was also carried to extremes. For example, the characters of Fletcherian tragicomedy often change from scene to scene, sacrificing dramatic consistency in order to elicit "the maximum emotional response" contained in every particular moment. Commenting on the characters of Beaumont and Fletcher, Dryden says "they are either good, bad, or indifferent, as the present scene requires it." The tendency to minimize overall significance for momentary effect is noticeable in many of the Jacobean plays, and by the Restoration heroic drama has become little short of operatic, employing set speeches like arias.

Since our object is to examine the exaggerated tendencies of the period, we shall turn to *The Rehearsal* for our account of the heroic play. According to Buckingham and his friends, the one aim of the heroic play is transport, at whatever cost. The search for novelty is epitomized by Bayes (the Dryden of *The Rehearsal*) when he says, "I'll do nothing here that ever was done before." All his fancies are "new," and he "would not have any two things alike in this play" (IV.1). Surprise is used for its own sake: "Here's an odd surprise," says Bayes; "all these dead men you shall see rise up presently, at a certain note that I have made, in *Effaut flat*, and fall a-dancing" (II.5). "Songs, ghosts, and dances," as well as whole scenes, are introduced irrelevantly into the play to "surprise" (III.1). Spectacle is accordingly a main objective, its most obvious form being size. Other characteristics of Bayes' play are complexity and plot and obscurity: "for to guess presently at the plot and the sense, tires [the audience] before the end of the first act" (I.2): and the play's epilogue remarks that "The play is at an end, but where's the plot? / That circumstance our poet Bayes forgot." The plot, in fact, never manages to get under way, the effect of Bayes' technique being a distortion of the whole for the sake of local effect and of the ideal for momentary transport.

It should be apparent by now that a general trend in the art of the seventeenth century was casuist or opportunist. Thus the digression, which destroys pattern on behalf of casual insight, becomes a prominent characteristic, and the most up-and-coming form is the essay — a tentative effort in some direction. Each of Dryden's prefaces embodies an attempt, Dryden's belief of the moment, but provides no overall structure of critical theory; and the ideas — for example, those concerning rhyme and blank verse — change from essay to essay. When he writes one, it represents the absolute truth of that moment; the next, though a reversal of opinion, will be as valid to him because it represents the truth of that moment, as he sees it.

The critical demigod of the last quarter of the century was "Longinus," another Silver Age figure, whom Dryden ranked next to Aristotle. It has been pointed out that the figures recommended by Longinus for achieving sublimity all "tend to have to do with abnormalities of syntax and other peculiarities of structure," and that "In the final analysis . . . the supreme quality of a work turns out to be the reflected quality of its author: — 'Sublimity is the echo of a great soul.' " The idiosyncratic and personal, the distorted and extravagant are to be used for "not persuasion but transport." Longinus talks of the "spell" imposing speech "throws over us," and emphasizes the "power and irresistible might" the sublime exerts over the reader, as well as the reader's loss of control. The neo-Longinian made "transport" into "enthusiasm" or "passion," which extended upward to religious experience. John Dennis — "Sir Longinus" as he was later called — felt the necessity for more emotion in poetry, a "fine frenzy" being the indispensable element. His solution was to infuse poetry with religious enthusiasm. From Longinus' theory and Milton's poetry he built a system which identified inspiration with passion and the highest poetry with the expression of religious enthusiasm. Dryden's own critical defense of the heroic mode brings out the Longinian elements clearly:

> And if any man object the improbabilities of a spirit appearing, or of a palace raised by magic: I boldly answer him, that an heroic poet is not tied to a bare representation of what is true, or exceeding probable; but that he may let himself loose to visionary objects, and to the representation of such things as depending not on sense, and therefore not to be comprehended by knowledge, may give him a freer scope for imagination.

Longinus has brought us back to the point we noticed in connection with Donne's apology for the Metaphysical style, that personal idiosyncrasy is raised to the level of a universal. As I said at the beginning of this section, we have developed one possible view of seventeenth-century forms of literature; we have looked at these supposed excesses from the point of view of the Restoration critics, of South, Glanvill, Eachard, and Marvell. But we can show that Swift agreed in general with these critics by glancing at the *Mechanical Operation of the Spirit*, where we find: "The Force, or Energy of this [modern] Eloquence, is not to be found, as among antient Orators, in the Disposition of Words to a Sentence, or the turning of long Periods; but agreeable to the Modern Refinements in Musick, is taken up wholly in dwelling, and dilating upon Syllables and Letters."

In other of his writings we learn that he admired the style of Elizabethans like Hooker and Parsons for its "Simplicity which is the best and truest Ornament of most Things in human Life" and distrusted the complexity, and consequent lack of clarity, in the style of anti-Ciceronians like Sir Henry Wotton. In his "Proposal for Correcting, Improving, and Ascertaining the English Tongue" (1711) he gives his account of literary history as regards prose style: "The period, wherein the English Tongue received most improvement, I take to commence with the beginning of Queen Elizabeth's reign, and to conclude with the great rebellion of forty-two. It is true, there was a very ill taste both of style and wit, which prevailed under King James the First." He believes this was corrected under Charles I (probably with the Laudian reform); but from the Civil War to the present, "I am apt to doubt, whether the corruptions in our language have not at least equalled the refinements of it; and these corruptions very few of the best authors in our age have wholly escaped. During the usurpation, such an infusion of enthusiastic jargon prevailed in every writing, as was not shaken off in many years after. To this succeeded that licentiousness which entered with the Restoration."

What he attacks here, with a National Academy for standardizing the language in mind, are the Puritan jargon, the shortening of words, the "affected phrases" of plays, and the irresponsible creation of new words. The general trend of his thought is evident: new words are created to express new and odd states of mind. In the matter of preaching, Swift followed St. Augustine's aims: "ut doceat, ut delectet, ut flectat" (teach, delight, move). In his "Letter to a Young Gentleman, Lately enter'd into Holy Orders" Swift makes it clear that teaching is the object of a sermon, and accordingly clarity and simplicity are the necessary qualities it must possess. "Where Men err against this Method," he says, "it is usually on Purpose, and to shew their Learning, their Oratory, their Politeness, or their Knowledge of the World."

In our survey of the seventeenth century, then, we have seen that such different forms as the sermon, the polemical pamphlet, and the heroic drama have much in common with the anatomies with which our discussion began. In all of these forms detail takes on a greater autonomy than is always consistent with the overall aim of the work, whether as a manifestation of the author's own individuality of purpose or as a device for moving the reader momentarily. There is a noticeable conflict between part and whole, each claiming the reader's undivided attention, and often not finally agreeing. In short, means—or method—may be said to have overwhelmed ends.

III. THE *TALE* AS PARODY

We began by assuming that the *Tale* bears resemblances to the seventeenth-century writings we have been discussing. It will be well, however, to demonstrate this fact briefly before going on to see what it may mean.

Anyone opening *A Tale of a Tub* must be struck by the apparently pointless piling up of introductory sections and the tendency of the digressions to swamp the tale of the three brothers, which is the ostensible subject. Most sentences demonstrate a conscious search for the asymmetrical, an avoidance of forethought, an employment of whatever happens to be at hand. Some sentences which sound most portentous, and bristle with shows of order, simply flow off into an endless linking of unsubordinated members. The unemphatic sentence shows a mode of progression that could be demonstrated as easily from paragraph to paragraph and from section to section. The *Tale's* preface, for example, moves from an explanation of the book's purpose and origin to a discussion of why the preface is not as long as modern prefaces should be, to an explanation of why the author has not attacked other writers, to clues as to how the reader should read the book, to a discussion of satire. The *Tale* itself wanders from critics to madmen in Bedlam, from discussions of prefaces to discussions of digressions.

The accumulation of information along the way—such as the account of the macrocephali, the white powder that kills without report, or the slitting of a stag's ear that spreads through a whole herd—suggests that Swift wants his book to recall a mound of erudition like Browne's *Pseudodoxia Epidemica*. We find here the same sprinkling of Latin and Greek, the same references to learned authorities, the same abstruse speculations we encounter in the anatomy. We find suggestions of all manner of seventeenth-century forms in the *Tale*. The tour of Bedlam in section 9 is a convention of many a Jacobean play, as is the idea of the alternating plot and subplot, narrative and digression. At the other end of the century we have the report of the Royal Society parodied in the report on oratorial machines and falling bodies (i.e. words) in the introduction, Restoration comedy parodied in the posturing fops of the allegory of the coats (section 2), and the etymological pursuits of the Bentleyan critic parodied in "A Digression concerning Criticks." Judging by the briefest look at the *Tale*, it is safe to say, with Herbert Davis, that "in its outward shape and form it obviously resembles the work of those writers whom Swift repudiates, rather than the work of those like Hooker and Parsons, whose style he admired." Swift admits in his "Author's Apology" appended to the fifth edition (1710) that there are, in the *Tale*, "what they call Parodies, where the Author personates the Style and Manner of other Writers, whom he has a mind to expose."

Like the seventeenth-century works we have examined, the *Tale* expresses a personal view of the universe; but it only *pretends* to be personal. It pretends to have "included and exhausted all that Human Imagination can *Rise* or *Fall* to." It pretends to demonstrate exhaustive learning. It pretends to be eccentric. It satirizes works like those we have noticed, and so itself offers an implicit analysis of eccentricity. In short, the *Tale* is *about* eccentricity rather than an example itself.

Swift's parody is built around the vehicle of his theme, his speaker. The queerness that is apparent in Swift's speaker has the same explanation as the other peculiarities we have noticed in the *Tale*: his mode of thought represents one aspect of the seventeenth-century sensibility. Having grasped the fact that the digressions and other eccentricities are manifestations of this sensibility, it is easier to see that one of the comic elements in the portrayal of the Grub Street Hack is his unabashed sacrifice of everything else for the effect of the moment—his willingness to collapse an argument for the sake of delicious details; or, in short, his casuistry. This aspect of the speaker is perhaps the key to the *Tale's* structure and to Swift's relationship to his material.

The word Swift uses to express his own relationship to the *Tale* is "Irony": "there generally runs an Irony through the Thread of the whole Book," he remarks in the "Author's Apology." Doubtless written as an answer to those who assumed Swift himself to be the speaker of the *Tale*, the remark itself is an ironic understatement. But it is, of course, possible to take sentiments like the refusal to "detract from the just Reputation of this famous Sect [the Aeolists]" as the speaker's irony rather than his wide-eyed sincerity. If we accepted this view, we should conclude that the Grub Street Hack is himself being satirical and is not an instrument of Swift's satire, that there is no appreciable distinction between his views and Swift's. It is also possible to take the *Tale* as a sort of dialogue between two speakers, Swift sometimes coming through in his own voice. It is a fairly common view that the "whiplash" of "Fool among Knaves" is Swift's momentary dropping of his mask. More common yet is the critic's implicit acceptance of Swift as himself associated with the metaphor of dissection. Craik is guilty of this implication when he speaks of Swift's "marvellous strength and grasp with which the whole of human nature is seized, bound to the dissecting table, and made to yield, to his pitiless scalpel, the tale of its subterfuges, and pretences, and tricks."

These views tend to lose their usefulness when we see that the Hack is an embodiment of the zeal, enthusiasm, and various kinds of eccentricity which he may *seem* to talk about satirically. The parts that disturb readers most, however, are the quick reversals and non sequiturs, the most famous of which is in the "Digression on Madness," where one minute the Hack attacks Reason for being a dissector with claws, "for cutting, and opening, and mangling, and piercing," and a few sentences later he is himself watching a woman flayed and ordering a beau stripped and dissected. The latter is, accordingly, often taken to be Swift intruding. The inconsistency appears in the Hack's using a method he has just attacked; but in terms of the moment in which he speaks the Hack's position is perfectly consistent: to prove his point, that the outside (appearance) is lovely and should not be removed to seek the nasty reality, which is inside, he has to reveal the inside. In the same way, he is hired to write against the wits who pick at the "weak sides of Religion and Government"; but he defends the critics who make "many useful Searches into the weak sides of the *Antients*." He can also attack these "penetrating" wits and praise the "penetrating Reader," or on one page defend the wits and on another attack them—one is on his side, one is not.

In both the preface and the introduction an image of a crowd of milling people appears. In the former, we are told that the fat man who pushes and shoves, trying to get more room for himself, is not polite; in the latter, getting above the crowd is considered an ideal and we are approvingly shown ways of achieving it. The difference is in the context: in the first he is speaking of himself as one of the crowd, in the second he is one of the orators himself. But while the contexts are different, the metaphor is the same—as it was with the metaphor of dissection—and this irony, wholly outside the Hack's awareness, reveals to the reader an aggressive tendency in the Hack which he may not have been so conscious of before.

At other times, like some of the seventeenth-century divines we have seen, he commits himself to a metaphor which, when its vehicle is carried out consistently, damages the tenor he is trying to convey. In the "Dedication to Prince Posterity" he chooses the metaphor of drowning for the modern books which have disappeared. " 'Tis certain," he says, "that in their own Nature they were *light* enough to swim upon the Surface for all Eternity." He is trying to prove that they would not naturally drown, by virtue of their own properties, and so he uses "light." But to keep his metaphor consistent he has admitted the lightness (i.e. superficiality) of his books. Elsewhere, when he finds it necessary to stress their sublimity, they are heavy, profound and deep; they make a reader "descend to the very *bottom* of all the *Sublime*."

In the same section he defeats an intended meaning in order to evoke the tone required at that moment. "Unhappy Infants," he cries, "many of them barbarously destroyed, before they have so much as learnt their *Mother-Tongue* to beg for Pity." He has brought about a tone of sentimental pathos, but he has ended by admitting that modern writers do not know their own language.

Whatever the moment calls for, the Hack uses, in spite of any general inconsistency. In fact, an obsessive quirk of the Hack's style is his referring repeatedly to the moment in which he is writing: "being just come from having the Honor conferred upon me," or "this Minute I am writing," or "the very Garret I am now writing in." More often verb tenses emphasize the present moment: "What *is* become of them?" not "what became (or even has become) of them?" And when he refers to the past it is with specific dates or times, as with "Last Week I saw a Woman *flay'd*," or "Yesterday I ordered the Carcass of a *Beau* to be stript." By holding change down to "Last Week" or "Yesterday" he is trying to impose some sort of order on experience, although by a misplaced emphasis he overlooks the forest for the trees.

This casuistry is a notable link between the Hack and the seventeenth-century sensibility. His whole world, we shall see, is characterized by complete reliance on the momentary effect, forgetfulness of all that went before or that will come after.

The idea of the persona is itself typically seventeenth-century. The anti-Ciceronian writer automatically sets up a persona in his writings, whether it is the man Montaigne, the prophet Milton, or the companionable abstraction of a Dryden essay. Here the unity of idea or form is replaced by the unity of a "personality," maintained from essay to essay. What is more comic than the mind searching for order and oneness, in terms of the changeableness of mood, prejudice, and even intention? Donne and Browne and a host of others sought this order, demonstrating the process of their discovery; but nobody before Swift seems to have noticed the incongruity of end and means.

We shall discuss [elsewhere] what principle directs the Hack's casuistry; but what these conflicting tendencies lead to in terms of the persona is an abstractness which tends to deny the Hack the individuality necessary if he is to be accepted as a fiction. There are points where the Hack's logic carries him to such an extreme of unawareness that the statement could be spoken as well by Swift. "But about this time it fell out, that the Learned Brother aforesaid, had read *Aristotelis Dialectica*, and especially that wonderful Piece *de Interpretatione*, which has the Faculty of teaching its Readers to find out a Meaning in every Thing but it self; like Commentators on the *Revelations*, who proceed Prophets without understanding a Syllable of the Text." The passage, like an optical illusion, can be seen in two altogether different ways, though the pattern remains the same. It can be seen as a direct statement of the author's view of the Bentleyan interpreter of texts; it can also be seen as the words of the Hack, whose values have become so inverted that commentators do not need to "understand a Syllable of the Text." The latter may be thought to show such fatuousness that the Hack tends to lose individuality. We may begin to think that there is some basic disagreement between the Hack and the reader on the meaning of words.

Whenever this coincidence takes place, it creates a moment of extraordinary intensity—for example, the "Fool among Knaves" statement—unlike the passages where the Hack's view must be corrected by a reference to common sense. But the result is that, in terms of the *Tale* as a work of art, the rhetorical effect of the moment sometimes blurs the over-all effect of the work; to this extent, some of the seventeenth-century casuistry may be thought to have rubbed off onto Swift himself.

Thus one of the facts about the *Tale* that contribute to its curiously unique air is that a reader is never wholly convinced of the fiction, nor unconvinced: if he were convinced, a passage like the above would be accepted without hesitation as the Hack's and enjoyed as such. But the Hack, in spite of all the details which can be shown to prove his psychological consistency and almost independent existence, never completely detaches himself from Swift. It is not easy to see why; but the critical evidence of two and a half centuries (discounting prejudice and willful misunderstanding) shows that most readers find the ambiguity there. I suspect that the reason is that he, unlike Lemuel Gulliver, is too symbolic, or doctrinaire, too much the apologist and not enough the autobiographer.

Therefore, the question which remains is the extent to which the eccentricity we have observed is in some way reordered by the *Tale* so as to receive perspective and criticism. We have seen already an indication of how that reordering can be done: while the Hack is concerned with his individual moments the reader who seeks consistency will put the moments together and arrive at some of the tentative meanings we have suggested in this section. In the next chapter we shall examine some ways of reordering and see what sort of a theme is implied by the relationship we are outlining between order and disorder.

MARTIN PRICE

Swift: Order and Obligation

In *Gulliver's Travels* Swift carries the conflict of orders to its sharpest expression. Lemuel Gulliver is the most famous of Swift's masks or personae, and, as always, it is important to see these masks in their fictional integrity first of all. Swift may not be consistent in maintaining them; they become at moments transparencies through which his irony shines in full intensity, but much of the nonsense that has been written about Swift's works derives from a failure to observe the character of their spokesmen. Gulliver is obtuse in a plausible and often attractive way. He is a matter-of-fact man, capable of minute accuracy of detail in what he reports but equally capable of total indifference to the "value tone" of experience. His deadpan style is consistent understatement through much of the book. It is not knowing understatement such as we find in Hemingway, conscious of all it refuses to mention. It is, rather, unconscious irony—a style that is calculated (by Swift and not by Gulliver) to reveal sharply just those values it fails to observe or mention; a style that gives itself away. Swift's spokesmen are always chosen for this useful service: they cheerfully systematize, they avow what is commonly suppressed, they scandalize where wiser or more cautious men would draw back and reconsider.

Gulliver is invented as the hero of a comedy of incomprehension. This is only one dimension of *Gulliver's Travels*, but it is an essential one. Why comedy rather than satire? Because, in this one dimension, Gulliver embodies the incorrigible tendency of the mind to oversimplify experience, a trait that takes, with equal ease, the form of complacency or of misanthropy. Given his tendency to see man as either a rational animal or an irrational beast, given his expectation

From *To the Palace of Wisdom*. © 1964 by Martin Price. Southern Illinois University Press, 1964.

that man will be essentially good or essentially evil, Gulliver can never comprehend the problematic nature of man as he really is. As Swift sees him, man is
both blessed and cursed with the condition of *animal rationis capax*. Because he
is capable of reason man can at least glimpse moral truth, because he is less than
perfect in it he can lose the vision or pervert its meaning. The book raises the
question of how much that we call civilization is an imperfect disguise of our
lowest appetites (rather than a true sublimation or transformation of them), and
also how far this civilization is necessary to the man who lives a purely moral life,
adhering rigorously to the precepts of nature and reason alone (revelation apart).
This is the same problem raised at least in passing by the *Argument against Abolishing Christianity.*

Finally, the book considers fundamental questions about the nature of politics, like the ideal reconciliation of duty and interest among the Houyhnhnms
and the less perfect, but more humanly feasible, reconciliation in Brobdingnag.
To these political orders are opposed such societies as that of the Lilliputians,
which is elaborately administered disorder, the tyrannies of Laputa and Mal-
donada, and the savage democracy of the Yahoos. *Gulliver's Travels* is a tribute
to the mixed state in which order is reconciled with freedom and yet made stable.
To achieve such an order, one must come to terms with the nature of power, and
the most essential feature of power is its tendency to become absolute.

Let us consider the political order. In Lilliput, Gulliver becomes the absolute
weapon of an Emperor whose only wish is to conquer the world (that his world
consists of two small islands makes the desire depressingly petty in its object but
hardly petty in its intensity). The "spirit of opposition" governs the world of
Lilliput; there is "a violent faction at home, and the danger [largely imaginary, a
self-induced terror which unites the state, as in Orwell's *1984*] of an invasion by
a most potent enemy from abroad" (I, iv). The occasions for dispute (like those
for conquest) are so trivial as to be meaningless; the power drive creates its own
pretexts. Within the state, the factions are rivals for influence and favor. Ministers are chosen by their agility—skill in walking a tightrope or jumping over
sticks—and their subservience. The language of the court is a constant exercise
in obfuscation. When the King's clemency is declared, his subjects run for cover.
When Gulliver hastily puts out the fire in the Empress' palace by the quickest
means available, the court accusation is a wonderful farrago of insinuation, self-
importance, and intolerable legal jargon:

> Whereas . . . it is enacted that whoever shall make water within the
> precincts of the royal palace shall be liable to the pains and penalties of
> high treason: notwithstanding, the said Quinbus Flestrin [i.e., Gul-
> liver], in open breach of the said law, under color of extinguishing
> the fire kindled in the apartment of his Majesty's most dear imperial

consort, did maliciously, traitorously, and devilishly, by discharge of his urine, put out the said fire kindled in the said apartment, lying and being within the precincts of the said royal palace, against the statute in that case provided, etc., against the duty, etc.

(I, vii)

Or again Gulliver is accused of preparing to make a voyage to Blefuscu, "for which he hath received only verbal licence from his Imperial Majesty."

What is even more telling than the crazy mock logic of Lilliputian politics is Gulliver's readiness to adapt to it. A bluff, well-meaning Englishman, twelve times their size and able to destroy them with ease, he becomes dazzled by the honors paid him and the high status he has won at court. Gulliver is restrained in part by oaths, in part by a sense of gratitude, but in part, too, by a naïve readiness to assume that power confers right. This becomes clear when, at the court of Brobdingnag, he reveals his belated schooling in Machiavellian statecraft and offers the horrified King the gift of gunpowder. Gulliver's disappointment at the rejection of this proposal is strong:

A strange effect of narrow principles and short views! That a prince . . . should from a nice, unnecessary scruple, whereof in Europe we can have no conception, let slip an opportunity put into his hands, that would have made him absolute master of the lives, the liberties, and the fortunes of his people.

(II, vii)

In contrast to Lilliput, the Brobdingnagians have laws of no more than twenty-two words, and "to write a comment upon any law is a capital crime." Instead of a professional army they have a citizen militia, where "every farmer is under the command of his own landlord, and every citizen under that of the principal men in his own city, chosen after the manner of Venice by ballot" (II, vii). The militia fixes power in the whole body of the people rather than permitting the army to become an uncontrollable bloc such as we know in Latin-American politics today, and controls the disease that has attacked Brobdingnag, as it has every other nation: "the nobility often contending for power, the people for liberty, and the King for absolute dominion."

In the land of the Houyhnhnms we find an anarchy of reasonable creatures, such as William Godwin admired. The rational horses need no government; they immediately intuit their duties and perform them. Only in a rare instance, where a novel situation is created—as by Gulliver's presence—must they deliberate. They control any dissidence by rational persuasion and "exhortation," for they need no compulsion. George Orwell is interesting but, I think, mistaken when he sees in this exhortation the "totalitarian tendency which is explicit in the

anarchist or pacifist vision of Society. In a Society in which there is no law, and
in theory no compulsion, the only arbiter of behavior is public opinion," —
which, Orwell shrewdly remarks, "is less tolerant than any system of law." This
might be true if the Houyhnhnms cultivated a "general will," or if they carried
on the kind of virtuous terrorism that in schools often goes by the name of
"honor system." But there is no need to exert "continuous pressure" for conformity among the Houyhnhnms. They cannot but agree in all but an occasional
matter, and even in the case Swift presents the Houyhnhnm master hesitates to
assent only because of Gulliver's furious resistance to being sent away. Other
critics have made similar objections about the religion of the Houyhnhnms. But
one cannot call them conformists, as Orwell does, or Deists, as others do. Their
reason inevitably produces agreement, and their piety is exemplary within the
limits of their purely natural reason. We cannot blame them for finding fulfill-
ment in what, for us, would be defects of liberty or failures of Christian faith.

The same kind of problem occurs in the realm of politics. Gulliver's account
    Why should Swift have created these problems for us? Clearly he is de-
manding of his readers what he never grants to Gulliver, the power to make necessary distinctions. We must separate the intuitive rightness of the Houyhnhnms'
choice from the tyranny of conformity, and we must separate natural piety from
rationalistic or anticlerical deism. Gulliver fails to make the most important distinction of all—between *animal rationale* and *animal rationis capax*. Only after
long exposure to human folly and perversity does he give up the dream of man as
a rational animal, but instead of coming to terms with what in fact he is, Gulliver immediately turns to truly rational animals, the Houyhnhnms, and hopes
to become one of them. His pathetic whinny and canter betray the fantasy of a
literal-minded convert.

The same kind of problem occurs in the realm of politics. Gulliver's account
of English institutions to the King of Brobdingnag betrays the corruptibility they
invite: English laws are extremely complex, and they "are best explained, interpreted, and applied by those whose interest and abilities lie in perverting, confounding, and eluding them" (II, vi). There is no reconciliation of duty and
interest, but instead a systematic perversion of duty by interest. In his account of
Europe to his Houyhnhnm master, Gulliver makes explicit all that he has earlier
unconsciously revealed. Lawyers are now "equally disposed to pervert the general
reason of mankind in every other subject of discourse, as in that of their own
profession" (IV, v). This single instance is typical of all the rest. Gulliver has
come to recognize the nature of corruption, but his recognition is so belated and
so passionate that he despairs of all politics. When he writes an account of his
travels, he expects the world to reform at once. But, in this case at least, we have
a third possibility firmly sketched in: the reformed mixed state of the Brobdingnagians, which mediates between duty and interest, conformity and freedom,
and accepts the need for a power structure but diffuses its control.

Parallel to the political issues in the book is the relationship of body and reason. In Lilliput, Gulliver's body is grosser than he can imagine (although he senses it), and the Lilliputians seem more delicate than in fact they are. In Brobdingnag the human body becomes monstrous, as Gulliver confronts with microscopic acuteness its ugliness and its noisome smells. In both the Struldbruggs and the Yahoos we see bodies that are completely without control or cleanliness; in fact, the Yahoos revel in filth and use excrement as a weapon. The body becomes a physical symbol of the power drives that are seen in the body politic; in Brobdingnag there is ugliness (simply more visible to Gulliver because of his diminutive size, as his own normal human ugliness was apparent to the Lilliputians) as there is cruelty and at least some measure of corruption (the farmer's turning Gulliver into a profitable show, the court dwarf's malice), but there is also a saving control of both corruption and physical nastiness. In the Struldbruggs old age has produced physical deterioration, avarice, contentiousness, and irrationality; in the Yahoos (who seem to have degenerated from an original couple, like the human race) there is sheer abandoned animality. The Yahoos are particularly nasty animals, it should be noted, not because Swift "in his fury . . . is shouting at his fellow-creatures: 'You are filthier than you are!' " (Orwell's view) but because they are a degenerate species, which neither possesses the instinctive controls of other animals (such as seasonal mating) nor preserves the faculties by which the human animal controls itself—its rational powers. Recent experiments have shown us animals that lose the power to identify with their proper kind and cannot acquire the traits of the kind they are raised among. Something of the sort has happened to the Yahoos; and their nastiness is only a further tribute to the importance of man's rational powers of self-control.

A third pattern, related to both politics and the control of the physical body, is that of simplicity and complexity. The Brobdingnagian laws are transparently simple; the Houyhnhnms need no laws at all. So it is with their cultures. The King, whose largeness of vision has the generosity of a Renaissance humanist, reminds us that Brobdingnag is a place of cultivation. But his people do not create books in great quantity; their largest library has a thousand volumes. In their writing "they avoid nothing more than multiplying unnecessary words, or using various expressions." They are skilled in practical arts, but utterly resistant to "ideas, entities, transcendentals, and abstractions." We see the reverse of this throughout the third voyage—the elaborate astronomy of Laputa is coupled with infantile superstition, the futile ingenuity of the experiments of Lagado is set against the simple adherence to traditional forms of Lord Munodi, the wisdom of Homer or Aristotle is swallowed up by the host of commentators that has battened on each. In place of the typical conqueror-heroes of history, Gulliver learns to admire the destroyers of tyrants and the defenders of liberty, the men who retrench corruption and win persecution in the process.

In the fourth voyage, the complexity of European civilization is traced in the Yahoos' savage behavior: they have a Prime Minister, they have court flirtations, they are acquisitive hoarders of shining stones, they become drunk and diseased, they even have a fashionable psychosomatic malady like the spleen. All the evils of civilization, and many of its professed glories, are caught in their elaborate behavior. In contrast, the Houyhnhnms perform "the necessary actions" of "a reasonable being" (IV, viii). They believe that "*reason* alone is sufficient to govern a *rational* creature"; they cannot even comprehend the nature of lies, let alone worse vices. "Neither is *reason* among them a point problematical as with us, where man can argue with plausibility on both sides of a question; but strikes you with immediate conviction, as it must needs do where it is not mingled, obscured, or discolored by passion and interest" (IV, viii). The consequences of perfect rational intuition are acute. They have no parental partiality nor do they mate except to bear children, and their choice of a marriage partner is based on cool eugenic principles. They accept death as natural ripeness and a return to the first mother. What are we to make of this passionless simplicity, where all is governed by the impartial virtues of friendship and benevolence?

In recent years critics have tended increasingly to find in the Houyhnhnms a satire upon the neo-Stoic humanism of Shaftesbury or the Deists. It is true that Swift mocks those who would base their lives on the belief that virtue is its own reward, but he does not mock the moral intuition that the Houyhnhnms live by. Of course, the Houyhnhnms are not human, and Swift never could have intended that we treat them as models. They are like that return to the System of the Gospels with which the *Argument against Abolishing Christianity* teases us. It would be disastrous to "our present schemes of wealth and power." But could we, in fact, return to primitive Christianity? In *A Tale of a Tub*, when the two brothers reject the corruptions introduced by the third, Jack performs a thorough reformation on his coat and tears it to shreds. Martin, on the other hand, preserves those additions that cannot be removed without destroying the fabric. So here, Swift mocks us with all we are not, with the simplicity and direct acceptance of obligation that is given all the more weight in the teaching of the Gospels (unknown to the merely "natural" Houyhnhnms), and with the close resemblance of our vaunted civilization to the bestiality of the Yahoos. But it is Gulliver, in his despair, who draws from this recognition the resolution to become a Houyhnhnm, and it is this that makes him shrink as if from a Yahoo when he encounters the generous and humane Portuguese sea captain who brings him back to Europe. At the last, even with his family, he is alienated, morose, contemptuous, although he has slowly begun to adapt himself once more to the human condition.

Swift is neither offering the Houyhnhnms as a model nor holding them up for satire. They have, it is true, some telltale complacency in the conclusions they draw without sufficient fact. But when Swift defends the ancient poets against ridicule, he points out that their moral teachings were altogether admirable within the limits of their awareness.

The Houyhnhnms would make a ludicrous model for man, but it is Gulliver who makes them that. They remain an embodiment—in alien animal form—of the life of unclouded moral intuition; a simple life because there are no passions to produce conflict or to generate "opinion." In most telling contrast to them is the Academy of Lagado, with its technical extravagance, its furious dedication to doing the unnecessary with the most dazzling ingenuity, its constant rediscovery of brute fact through ludicrous failure. The scientist who places the bellows to the posterior of a dog and inflates the beast until it explodes in a torrent of excrement serves as a link between the learning of Lagado and the filth of the Yahoos.

The Houyhnhnms represent the order of mind at its purest, free of rationalistic system-building or of pride in intellectual constructions. Conceived in this way, it contains much that is given to humans only in the order of charity—a moral sureness and serenity, a spontaneous goodness such as is bred in men by a "daily vision of God." But to achieve the equivalent in the world of men requires the arduous self-scrutiny, the courageous defiance of the world, the saving humility that Pope seeks to dramatize in the *Imitations of Horace*.

PAUL FUSSELL

The Paradox of Man

Man is thus a mighty curious creature. A flesh-machine of self-destructive depravity fraught with ignorance and vanity, and at the same time inspirited somehow with an *anima* which has it in its power to redeem all defects except, perhaps, mortality, he is a wandering paradox perpetually looking for a place now to hide and now to exhibit himself. He both is and is not like an angel; he both is and is not like a brute. It is his curse and his glory to be at home in a curious moral geography, "this isthmus of a middle state," as Pope puts it in the *Essay on Man*; and it is his nature that finally it can be suggested only by a series of the most outrageous paradoxes:

> A being darkly wise, and rudely great:
> With too much knowledge for the Sceptic side,
> With too much weakness for the Stoic's pride,
> He hangs between;

Perpetually in doubt, he can commit himself entirely to neither direction in which his dualistic being seems to invite him:

> in doubt to act, or rest,
> In doubt to deem himself a God, or Beast;
> In doubt his Mind or Body to prefer,

—and at this point in Pope's exhibition the pathos which is the usual attendant of the humanist view of man wells up:

> Born but to die, and reas'ning but to err;

From *The Rhetorical World of Augustan Humanism*. © 1965 by Oxford University Press.

Knowledge is of very little use in pointing to a satisfactory direction:

> Alike in ignorance, his reason such,
> Whether he thinks too little, or too much:

There is additional pathos in man's imagining himself "rational" and orderly, when actually he is only rarely even *capax rationis* and more often is simply a

> Chaos of Thought and Passion, all confus'd;

and whether in a state of ignorance or enlightenment, always his own worst enemy:

> Still by himself abus'd, or disabus'd;

His situation in the general hierarchy of things is both tense and tenuous:

> Created half to rise, and half to fall;

As Adam learns before his Fall, he is the "Great Lord of all things," and yet, as he discovers just after it, he is "a prey to all." In short, he is the "Sole judge of Truth," but he is also "in endless Error hurl'd." Small wonder that to the humanist he is at once

> The glory, jest, and riddle of the world!
>   (ii, 2–18)

After this demonstration of Pope's, it seems natural that the humanist, when contemplating man, will not know whether to laugh or to weep, and so will do both at once, as at the end of *Gulliver's Travels* or at the end of *The Dunciad*. Pope's version of man sounds familiar and even stale, but one reason why it does is that it occupies so central a position in human experience and in humanistic expression. Pope's "isthmus" recalls preeminently Hamlet's "sterile promontory," and Hamlet proceeds to lesson Rosencrantz and Guildenstern in a proto-Popian version of man which their mechanistic simplifications show them to be in need of:

> this most excellent canopy, the air, look you, this brave o'erhanging
> firmament, this majestical roof fretted with golden fire—why, it ap-
> peareth no other thing to me than a foul and pestilent congregation
> of vapours.

Warming to his humanist theme, he proceeds to sketch such a paradoxical picture of man's dualistic capacities that we wonder whether we are being "abus'd, or disabus'd":

> What a piece of work is a man! how noble in reason! how infinite in
> faculties! in form and moving how express and admirable! in action

> how like an angel! in apprehension how like a god! the beauty of the
> world! the paragon of animals!

And yet:

> And yet to me what is this quintessence of dust?
>
> (II, ii)

But familiar as it is, the paradox of the angelic brute is still capable of giving
pause, as it does to poor slow-witted Parson Adams in *Joseph Andrews*. The
parson's son Dick is reading the story about "Lennard's" wife: " 'But, good as
this lady was, she was still a woman; that is to say, an angel, and not an angel.' —
'You must mistake, child' cries the parson, 'for you read nonsense.' 'It is so in the
book,' answered the son." This paradoxical wise child owes something to a fusion
of classical and Christian motifs, suggesting at once the image of the blind Tiresias
being led by a boy and the Christian imagery of the innocent child leading the
dull adults.

The cause of paradox is the juxtaposition of all but irreconcilable dualisms.
This is the burden of Erwin Panofsky's definition of "humanism," which he locates in "man's proud and tragic consciousness of self-approved and self-imposed
principles, contrasting with his utter subjection to illness, decay and all that is
implied in the word 'mortality.' " It seems illuminating that the humanistic dual
view of man as at once angel and beast appears allied to the paradox of satire in
general. Perhaps more than any other kind of literature, satire transmits a dualistic vision, for it offers us always a surface of contempt, disparagement, and
ridicule masking something quite different, namely, an implicit faith in man's
capacity for redemption through the operation of choice. Satire works by taxing its
targets with brutishness in order to turn them angelward. In the Augustan instinct
for satire as a favourite literary action we can sense very powerfully the presence
of the dualistic vision of man which in varying degrees informs all humanist
literature of whatever age.

To those aware of the workings of the moral imagination, dualistic feelings
are inescapable, for, as Johnson writes in *Rambler* 169, "In proportion as perfection is more distinctly conceived, the pleasure of contemplating our own perfor-
mances will be lessened." And it seems to be the strength of his dualistic instinct
that keeps Johnson's view of man, even when highly satiric in tendency, from
ever turning into a mere Mandevillian cynicism. Thus he writes his friend John
Ryland: "As a being subject to so many wants Man has inevitably a strong tendency to self-interest, so I hope as a Being capable of comparing good and evil
he finds something to be preferred in good, and is, therefore, capable of benevolence. . . . " The subtlety and tenuousness of Johnson's mode of Christianity is
also provided in part by his dualistic habit. He suggests to Mrs. Thrale that "It
is good to speak dubiously about futurity. It is likewise not amiss to hope."

It would be hard to find a happier emblem of the humanist dualistic conception of man than the Master Houyhnhnm's solution to the problem of Gulliver's most appropriate lodging-place during his first night in Houyhnhnmland. Gulliver could be sent to harbour with the Yahoos, for he certainly looks rather like one; or he could remain in the house of the Houyhnhnms, for he is capable of a form of converse with them. What to do? Gulliver's master determines a meaningful compromise: "When it grew towards Evening, the Master Horse ordered a Place for me to lodge in; it was but Six Yards from the House, and separated from the Stable of the *Yahoos*. Here I got some Straw, and covering myself with my own Cloaths, slept very sound." This characteristically empirical, positional image locates Gulliver just where he belongs, in his proper "middle state" from which he is free to move in either direction. It is as if Swift were mindful of the ancient centaur myth and bent on domesticating it within the homely eighteenth-century realities and "comforts." Geoffrey Scott observes that what "nature" means to the humanist is not what it means to the savage nor yet what it means to the scientist. Taking Yahoos as loosely expressive of savagery and Houyhnhnms of science—perhaps their want of wit qualifies them, at least —we can see that what Scott says about the humanist's relation to "nature" illuminates Gulliver's challenge in Houyhnhnmland, the challenge that he accepts but bungles so badly. After positing a savage's "nature" and a scientist's "nature," Scott goes on to suggest that "a third way is open. [The humanist] may construct, within the world as it is, a pattern of the world as he would have it. This is the way of humanism, in philosophy, in life, and in the arts." But it is just this "third way" that Gulliver fails to take, a way which would make a gesture towards reconciling the dualistic extremes with which he is presented. Given his choice of behaving like the generous Captain Pedro de Mendez who rescues him or like the coherent, stable Martin of *A Tale of a Tub*, he decides instead to play a version of Peter, and the crashing irony is that he ends a slavering Jack. As Pope says in the *Essay on Man*, poor man is

> This hour a slave, the next a deity.
>
> (i, 68)

Gulliver sails proudly for home determined to act the deity, and succeeds only in turning slave.

Two-directional imagery like this image of Gulliver's lodging we encounter very frequently in Swift, and within the humanist tradition it seems the most common method for embodying ethical issues. Once we call it something like the habit of moral antithesis, it is obvious how it naturally works to shape the conventions of Augustan sentence structure and the syntactical and prosodic habits of the heroic couplet. Pope's prefatory remarks to the *Essay on Man* ("The Design") illustrate the dualistic or antithetical habit in prose: "If I could flatter myself that this Essay has any merit, it is in steering betwixt the extremes of doctrines seemingly opposite, . . . in forming a *temperate* yet not *inconsistent*, and a *short* yet not *imperfect* system of Ethics." Pope seems remarkably sensitive to the conventional halving of prayers in epic poetry, and his dualistic habit of mind seems to move him to recover the image for his own narrative uses. Thus in *The Rape of the Lock*

> [Lord Petre] begs with ardent Eyes
> Soon to obtain, and long possess the Prize:
> The pow'rs gave Ear, and granted half his Pray'r,
> The rest, the Winds dispers'd in empty Air.
>
> (ii, 43–46)

And complimenting Martha Blount in *Moral Essay* II, Pope tells her that Phoebus

> Averted half your Parents simple Pray'r,
> And gave you Beauty, but deny'd the Pelf
> That buys your sex a Tyrant o'er itself.
>
> (286–88)

The theme of human limitations is admirably "incorporated" by Swift in the image of the frailty of Gulliver's body. Indeed, it is remarkable what happens physically to poor Gulliver during his four voyages. He does far more suffering than acting. Even though as a surgeon he is more likely than most to dwell obsessively on his own physical injuries, and even though his commitment to the ideals of the Royal Society impels him to deliver his narrative with a comically detailed circumstantiality, he records a really startling number of hurts. In the voyage to Lilliput, for example, his hair is painfully pulled, and his hands and face are blistered by needle-like arrows. During his stay among the people of Brobdingnag he is battered so badly that he appears almost accident-prone: his flesh is punctured by wheat-beards; twice his sides are painfully crushed; he is shaken up and bruised in a box; his nose and forehead are grievously stung by flies as big as larks; he suffers painful contusions from a shower of gigantic hailstones; he "breaks" his shin on a snailshell; and he is pummelled about the head and body by a linnet's wings. And during his fourth voyage he is brought again into dire physical jeopardy: his final series of physical ordeals begins as his hand is painfully squeezed by a horse. Finally, as he leaves Houyhnhnmland, Swift contrives that Gulliver shall suffer a wholly gratuitous arrow wound on the inside of his left knee ("I shall carry the Mark to my Grave"). Looking back on the whole extent of Gulliver's experiences before his final return to England, we are hardly surprised that his intellectuals at the end have come unhinged: for years his body has been beaten, dropped, squeezed, lacerated, and punctured. When all is said, the experiences which transform him from a fairly bright young surgeon into a raging megalomaniac have been almost as largely physical as intellectual and psychological. So powerfully does Swift reveal Gulliver's purely mental difficulties at the end of the fourth voyage that we may tend to forget that Gulliver has also been made to undergo the sorest physical trials. During the four voyages he has been hurt so badly that, although he is normally a taciturn, unemotional, "Roman" sort of person, he has been reduced to weeping three times; so severely has he been injured at various times that at least twenty-four of his total travelling days he has spent recuperating in bed.

In addition to these actual injuries which Gulliver endures, he also experiences a number of narrow escapes, potential injuries, and pathetic fears of physical hurt. In Lilliput the vulnerability of his eyes is insisted upon: an arrow barely misses his left eye, and only his spectacles prevent the loss of both his eyes as he works to capture the Blefuscan fleet. Furthermore, one of the Lilliputian punishments decreed for Quinbus Flestrin is that his eyes be put out. And during the Brobdingnagian trip Gulliver's experience is one of an almost continuous narrow escape from serious injury. He almost falls from the hand of the farmer and off the edge of the table. Stumbling over a crust, he falls flat on his face and barely escapes injury. After being held in a child's mouth, he is dropped, and he is saved only by being miraculously caught in a woman's apron. He is tossed into a bowl of cream, knocked down but not badly hurt by a shower of falling apples, and clutched dangerously between a spaniel's teeth. He is lucky to escape serious injury during a nasty tumble into a mole hill, whereupon he "coined some Lye not worth remembering, to excuse my self for spoiling my Cloaths." And during the sojourn at Laputa, he is afraid of some "hurt" befalling him in his encounter with the magician.

But Gulliver, who acts like a sort of physically vulnerable Ur-Boswell on the Grand Tour, is not the only one in the book who suffers or who fears injury: the creatures he is thrown among also endure catastrophes of pain and damage, often curiously particularized by Swift. Thus in Lilliput, two or three of the rope-dancers break their limbs in falls. A horse, slipping part way through Gulliver's handkerchief, strains a shoulder. The grandfather of the Lilliputian monarch, it is reported, as a result of breaking his egg upon the larger end suffered a cut finger. In the same way, the fourth voyage seems busy with apparently gratuitous details of injury and pain: for example, Gulliver carefully tells us that an elderly Houyhnhnm "of Quality" alighted from his Yahoo-drawn sledge "with his Hindfeet forward, having by Accident got a Hurt in his Left Forefoot."

Nor are all the manifold injuries in Gulliver's Travels confined to the bodies of Gulliver and his hosts. Gulliver's clothing and personal property suffer constant damage, and when they are not actually being damaged, Gulliver is worrying that at any moment they may be hurt. We are not surprised that a shipwrecked mariner suffers damage to his clothing and personal effects, but we are surprised that Gulliver constantly goes out of his way to call attention to the damages and losses he suffers: his scimitar, his hat, his breeches—all are damaged in Lilliput, and the damage is punctiliously recounted. In Brobdingnag the familiar process of damage and deterioration begins all over again: a fall into a bowl of milk utterly spoils Gulliver's suit; his stockings and breeches are soiled when he is thrust into a marrow bone; and his suit—what's left of it—is further ruined by being daubed with frog slime and "bemired" with cow dung. In the third voyage our attention is invited to the fact that his hat has again worn out, and in the fourth voyage we are told yet again by Gulliver that his clothes are "in a declining Condition."

Gulliver's clothes and personal effects, in fact, at times seem to be Gulliver himself: this is the apparent state of things which fascinates the Houyhnhnm before whom Gulliver undresses; and this ironic suggestion of an equation between Gulliver and his clothing, reminding us of the ironic "clothes philosophy" of section II of A Tale of a Tub, Swift exploits to suggest that damage to Gulliver's frail garments is the equivalent of damage to the frail Gulliver. The vulnerability of Gulliver's clothing, that is, is a symbol three degrees removed from what it appears to signify: damage to the clothes is symbolic of damage to the body; and damage to the body is symbolic of damage to Gulliver's complacent self-esteem.

These little incidents of injury and destruction are pervasive in *Gulliver's Travels*, as we are reminded by the recurrence—very striking once we are attuned to it—of words like "hurt," "injury," "damage," "accident," "mischief," "misfortune," and "spoiled." When we focus on what is happening physically in *Gulliver's Travels*, we sense the oblique presence of this motif of frailty and vulnerability even in passages which really address themselves to something quite different. For example: "His Majesty [the Emperor of Blefuscu] presented me . . . with his Picture at full length, which I immediately put into one of my Gloves, to keep it from being hurt." It is as if Swift were determined not to let us forget that there is a pathetic fragility in all his fictional objects, whether animate or inanimate.

And Swift seems to have provided within his text a key to these pervasive reminders of the vulnerability of man and the fragility of his personal effects. In the second voyage, we are told in a voice which sounds perhaps more Swiftian than Gulliverian of a "little old Treatise" treasured now only by elderly women and the more credulous vulgar, a copy of which Glumdalclitch has been given by her governess. The burden of this mysterious little book, we are told, is precisely the theme of the physical frailty of man: the book shows "how diminutive, contemptible, and helpless an Animal . . . [is] Man in his own Nature." Like Johnson's version of Juvenal in *London*, the book emphasizes man's liability to accident and injury; it argues that "the very Laws of Nature absolutely required we should have been made in the Beginning, of a Size more large and robust, not so liable to Destruction from every little Accident of a Tile falling from an House, or a Stone cast from the Hand of a Boy, or of being drowned in a little Brook." Here Swift appears to avail himself of the myth of the Decay of Nature as a fictional surrogate for the Christian myth of the Fall. Although, as Miss Kathleen Williams reminds us, Godfrey Goodman's *The Fall of Man, or the Corruption of Nature* (1616) is perhaps the kind of "little old Treatise" Swift has in mind, I think we shall not go far wrong if we associate—even though we do not identify —Glumdalclitch's conservative little book with the Bible itself. The theme that Swift realizes by means of the image of Gulliver's physical frailty appears quintessentially humanistic: the theme is the inadequacy of an unassisted self-esteem in redeeming man from his essential frailties of mind and spirit. Swift's conception of Gulliver is close to Pope's feeling for the China jar which is Belinda. And Pope's sense of human frailty in the *Essay on Man* reminds us of Gulliver's fear for his eyes in Lilliput and for his body in Brobdingnag: addressing "Presumptuous Man," Pope taxes him with being "so weak, so little, and so blind." In one of its most significant moods the Augustan humanist mind conceives of man thus as a little delicate cage of bones and skin constantly at the mercy of accidental damage or destruction.

Johnson's sense of man's littleness is such that, if Swift had not already written it, he might himself have been tempted to sketch such a comedy of man diminished as Gulliver enacts in his second voyage. Boswell reports:

> I mentioned that I was afraid to put into my journal too many little incidents. JOHNSON. "There is nothing, Sir, too little for so little a creature as man. It is by studying little things that we attain the great art of having as little misery and as much happiness as possible."

What Gulliver appears not to learn during his stay with the Brobdingnagians Johnson, in *Idler* 88, indicates that he has mastered completely: "a little more than nothing is as much as can be expected from [man], who with respect to the multitudes about him is himself little more than nothing." We think of the preposterousness of poor, foolish Gulliver who imagines that he is doing a great thing in performing on the spinet before the King and Queen of Brobdingnag, pounding on the keys with "two round Sticks about the Bigness of common Cudgels." Says Gulliver: "I ran sideling . . . that way and this, as fast as I could, banging the proper Keys with my two Sticks; and made a shift to play a Jigg to the great Satisfaction of both their Majesties." We may be forgiven if we impute their Majesties' "Satisfaction" more to their sense of the ridiculous than to their sense of wonder. Writing Boswell in 1777, Johnson speaks as an educated and redeemed Gulliver when he refers to the *Lives of the Poets* this way: "I am engaged to write little Lives, and little Prefaces, to a little edition of the English Poets." In short, man's ethical obligation is to learn "how to become little without becoming mean . . ." (*Rambler* 152).

CLAUDE RAWSON

Order and Cruelty:
A Reading of Swift (with some
comments on Pope and Johnson)

Swift's satire often suggests an impasse, a blocking of escape routes and saving possibilities. This feeling presses on the reader for reasons which do not necessarily follow from the satiric topic as such, from the specific wickedness Swift is castigating, or any outright assertion that the wickedness is incurable. Incurability is certainly often implied, and the sense of an impasse is (by a paradox which is only apparent) related to a complementary vision of unending paths of vicious self-complication, bottomless spirals of human perversity. This is less a matter of Swift's official ideological views than of mental atmosphere and ironic manipulation: that is, of a more informal, yet very active, interplay between deliberate attacking purposes (and tactics), and certain tense spontaneities of self-expression. My concern is with the stylistic results of this interplay, though I do not pretend that the deliberate purposes can be clearly distinguished from the more shadowy ones. It may be that in Swift such dividing lines *need* to be unclear. I begin with Swift's most frequently discussed passage, the mock-argument

> that in most Corporeal Beings, which have fallen under my Cognizance, the *Outside* hath been infinitely preferable to the *In*: Whereof I have been farther convinced from some late Experiments. Last Week I saw a Woman *flay'd*, and you will hardly believe, how much it altered her Person for the worse. Yesterday I ordered the Carcass of a *Beau* to be stript in my Presence; when we were all amazed to find so many unsuspected Faults under one Suit of Cloaths: Then I laid open his *Brain*, his *Heart*, and his *Spleen*; But, I plainly perceived at

From *Essays in Criticism* 20, no. 1 (January 1977). © 1970 by *Essays in Criticism*.

every Operation, that the farther we proceeded, we found the Defects
encrease upon us in Number and Bulk: from all which, I justly formed
this Conclusion to my self; That . . . He that can with *Epicurus* content his Ideas with the *Films* and *Images* that fly off upon his Senses
from the *Superficies* of Things; Such a Man truly wise, creams off
Nature, leaving the Sower and the Dregs, for Philosophy and Reason
to lap up. This is the sublime and refined Point of Felicity, called,
the Possession of being well deceived; The Serene Peaceful State of
being a Fool among Knaves.

(Tale of a Tub, IX)

Here, the example of the flayed woman supports an argument similar to
that of *A Beautiful Young Nymph Going to Bed*: whores can look horrible when
their finery is stripped off, conventional celebrations of female beauty gloss over
some ugly facts, the *Outside* looks better than the *In* and creates inappropriate
complacencies. The flayed woman is portrayed in less detail, and seems physically less shocking, than the nymph of the poem, with her artificial hair, eyes
and teeth, and her "Shankers, Issues, running Sores." But she is, in a sense, more
"gratuitous." In the poem, however horrible the details, the main proposition is
sustained by them in a manner essentially straightforward, formulaic, and indeed
conventional. The account is a nightmare fascination, but it is also simply a
donnée: the poem asks us to imagine such a woman, and the point is made.
The nymph is entirely subordinated to obvious formulaic purposes, even though
"subordination," in another sense, ill describes the vitality of the grotesquerie.

The flayed woman (and stripped beau), on the other hand, are momentary
intensities which do not merely *serve* the argument they are meant to illustrate,
but actually *spill over* it. They take us suddenly, and with devastating brevity,
outside the expectations of the immediate logic, into a surprising and "cruel"
domain of fantasy. "Cruel" is here used in something like Artaud's sense, as lying
outside or beyond ordinary moral motivations, and Swift's brevity is essential to
the effect. For this brevity, and the astringent blandness of the language, arrest
the play of fantasy sufficiently to prevent it from developing into a moral allegory
in its own right. The point is important, because brevity is not a necessary condition of a literature of cruelty in the modern sense, of Sade, Jarry and post-
Artaud dramatists, of Breton's *humour noir* and allied literary explorations of the
"gratuitous." When Breton placed Swift at the head of his anthology, as *véritable
initiateur* of a black humour emancipated from the "degrading influence" of satire
and moralising, he told a real truth, for Swift has (I believe) a temperamental
tendency in this direction. But the tendency is powerfully held in check by conscious moral purposes which harness it to their own use. Hence his gratuitous

cruelties are usually brief eruptions, only as long (so to speak) as the Super-Ego takes to catch up, and any extensive development of a grim joke normally dove-tails into a fully fledged moral demonstration or argument, as in the *Beautiful Young Nymph* or the *Modest Proposal*. Brief quasi-cannibalistic frissons in *Gulliver* (Gulliver using the skins of Yahoos for making clothes or sails, *GT*, IV. iii.) are more gratuitous than the *Modest Proposal*, as the flayed woman is more gratuitous than the *Beautiful Young Nymph* The *Gulliver* passages are extremely minor comic assaults on our "healthy" sensibilities, lacking the intensity of the passage from the *Tale*; but in one paradoxical sense they also are more unsettling than the more extended use of the cannibal image, precisely because in the *Proposal* the image is the direct sustaining principle of a moral argument. To this extent Breton seems off the mark when he follows his Swift section (which includes a substantial portion of the *Proposal*) with an elaborate cannibal ex-travaganza from Sade.

This is not to say that the briefer passages have no moral implication (nor that the extended ones lack the power to shock, or have no local and subsidiary intensities of their own). Presumably the clothes of Yahoo-skin are also a re-minder of the animality of man, while the flayed woman purports to illustrate the notion that appearances are more agreeable than reality. But it would take a per-verse reader to feel that these moral implications provide the dominant effect. The gruesomeness of the flayed woman is so shockingly and absurdly *over*-appropriate to the ostensible logic as to be, by any normal standards, *in*appropriate. Critics who recognise this sometimes sentimentalise the issue by arguing that the flayed woman overspills the immediate moral not into an amoral gratuitousness, but into a different and more powerful moral significance: that she represents, for example, Swift's pained protest at this treatment of whores. This seems as wrong as William Burroughs's notion that the *Modest Proposal* is "a tract against Capi-tal Punishment." I doubt Swift's opposition to either oppression, and if anything the allusion to flaying bears comparison with this sudden *redirection* of the can-nibal irony in the *Modest Proposal*:

> Neither indeed can I deny, that if the same Use were made of several plump young girls in this Town, who, without one single Groat to their Fortunes, cannot stir Abroad without a Chair, and appear at the *Play-house*, and *Assemblies* in foreign Fineries, which they never will pay for; the Kingdom would not be the worse.

In both cases the black joke suggests, if not literal endorsement of the hideous punishment, a distinct animus against the victim. The presence of this animus indicates that the irony is not, after all, gratuitous in the strictest Gide-ian sense. No human act can be entirely gratuitous (that is, absolutely motiveless), as Gide himself admitted: it can only be disconnected from its normal *external* functions, in this case the moral implications expected of the satire. If in both cases the animus is transferred suddenly away from the official paths of the formula (truth vs. delusion; eating people is wrong), yet still carries a redirected moral charge (against whores, or foolish girls whose vanity is crippling Ireland's economy), there is an explosive overplus in the sheer wilful suddenness of the act of redirection as such. A haze of *extra* hostility hangs in the air, unaccounted for, dissolving the satire's clean logic into murkier and more unpredictable precisions, spreading uneasiness into areas of feeling difficult to rationalise, and difficult for the reader to escape. Part of Swift's answer to the dilemma posed for the satirist by his own belief that "*Satyr is a sort of* Glass, *wherein Beholders to generally discover every body's Face but their own*" (*Battle of the Books*, preface) is thus to counter, by a strategy of unease, the reader's natural tendency to exclude himself from the explicit condemnation: his escape into "Serene Peaceful States" is blocked off even when he is innocent of the specific charge.

Often in such cases, moreover, the irony is manipulated in such a way as to suggest that the reader cannot be wholly unimplicated even in the specific charge. It is not only through unexpectedness or diversionary violence that the flayed woman and stripped beau spill over the logical frame. They also have an absurd tendency to generalise or extend the guilt to the rest of mankind, through a tangle of implications which act in irrational defiance of any mere logic. If the argument had been overridingly concerned to demonstrate that appearances can be fraudulent, superficial views inadequate, and vanity misplaced, the notion that people look ugly when stripped of their clothes or cosmetics would have been a sufficient, and a logically disciplined, support to it. To specify whores and beaux would be a perfectly legitimate singling out of social types who trade disreputably on appearances, and are otherwise open to moral censure. These didactic reasonings, and the larger-scale exposure of mad "moderns," obviously remain present. But, in the wording as it stands, they are also, characteristically, subverted; as though the several wires crossed, making an explosive short-circuit. Flayed or dissected bodies hardly produce the most morally persuasive evidence of the delusiveness of appearances; nor do they as such prove a moral turpitude. If a whore's body alters for the worse when flayed, or a beau's innards look unsavoury when laid open, so would anyone else's, and the fact does not obviously demonstrate anybody's wickedness. The images, which begin as specific tokens of guilt aimed at certain human types, teasingly turn into general signs of the human condition. The images' strong charge of undifferentiated blame is thus left to play over undefined turpitudes attributable to the whole of mankind. The beau's innards recall an earlier statement by the *Tale*'s "author," about having

dissected the Carcass of *Humane Nature*, and read many useful Lec-
tures upon the several Parts, both *Containing* and *Contained*; till at
last it *smelt* so strong, I could preserve it no longer.

(Tale, V)

The passage parodies Wotton and others, but, as often with Swiftian parody,
transcends its immediate object. And the imagery's characteristic oscillation between moral turpitude and bodily corruption irrationally suggests a damaging
equivalence between the two, placing on "*Humane Nature*" a freewheeling load
of moral guilt which is inescapable and which yet attaches itself to faults outside
the moral domain.

For if satire that is "levelled at all" (i.e., "general" rather than "personal")

is never resented for an offence by any, since every individual Person
makes bold to understand it of others, and very wisely removes his
particular Part of the Burthen upon the shoulders of the World, which
are broad enough, and able to bear it,

(Tale, preface)

this is only likely to be true of a "general" satire of *specific* vices. Where the
aggression turns indistinct, and overspills the area of specifiable moral guilt, no
opportunity is given for complacent self-exculpation on a specific front, and the
reader becomes implicated. Instead of permitting the individual to shift his load
onto the world's shoulders, Swift forces the reader to carry the world's load on
his. The result, second time round, is that even the specific charges begin to stick:
we become identified with whores, beaux, moderns. We cannot shrug this off by
saying that it is Swift's "author" who is speaking and not Swift. The intensities
are Swift's, and depend on the blandness and even friendliness of the "author."
The "author" is saying in effect *hypocrite lecteur, mon semblable, mon frère*,
and saying it kindly and welcomingly; but it is Swift who is making him say it,
and the reader must decide whether he likes the thought of such a brother.

The cumulative sense of impasse (all mankind becoming implicated in the
attack, the attack surviving any dismissal of specific charges, the curious revali-
dation of these charges by that fact, the miscellaneous blocking of the reader's
escape-routes) depends, then, on energies which exceed the legitimate logical
implications of the discourse. These energies cannot be accounted for by a mere
retranslation of the mock-logic into its non-ironic "equivalent," and part of their
force depends on the violation of whatever consequential quality exists either in
the hack's zany reasoning or its sober didactic counterpart. The carefully and
extensively prepared polarity between the mad values of the modern hack, and

the sanity of the non-singular, traditionalist, rational, unsuperficial man of sense, may seem for a while, in the Digression on Madness, solid and definite enough to provide at least limited reassurance against the more unsettling stylistic tremors. The reassurance is undermined but perhaps not eliminated by the flayed woman and stripped beau. But in the final sentence of the paragraph, the bad and good cease to function in lines that are parallel and opposite: the lines collapse, and cross. The comforting opposition is brought to a head, and then shattered, against the whole direction of the argument, by the suggestion that the alternative to being a fool is to be not a wise man but a knave.

Critics often assume some form of "diametrical opposition" between puta-tive and real authors at this point. Either Swift's voice suddenly erupts, nakedly, from the other's vacuous chatter, or at best "fools" and "knaves" have simulta-neously one clear value for Swift and an opposite one for his "author." I suggest that the relationship is at all times more elusive, and that the rigidities of mask-criticism (even in its more sophisticated forms) tend to compartmentalise what needs to remain a more fluid and indistinct interaction. (The theoretically clear opposition, in the preceding part of the Digression, between mad and sane, or bad and good, is a different thing: a temporary buildup, created for demolition.) The notion that in the "Fool among Knaves" we suddenly hear Swift's own voice makes a kind of sense: but it runs the danger of suggesting quite improperly both that we have not actively been hearing this voice throughout, and that we now hear nothing else. In actual fact, the phrase trades simultaneously on our feeling that the sudden intensity comes straight from Swift, and on our reluctance to identify Swift even momentarily with an "author" whom the work as a whole relentlessly ridicules. The paradox of that "author" is that he has enormous vitality, a "presence" almost as insistent as Swift's, without having much defin-able *identity* as a "character." He needs to be distinguished from Swift, but hardly as a separate and autonomous being. He is an ebullient embodiment of many of Swift's dislikes, but the ebullience is Swift's, and the "author" remains an amor-phous mass of disreputable energies, whose vitality belongs less to any indepen-dent status (whether as clear-cut allegory or full-fledged personality) than to an endlessly opportunistic subservience to the satirist's needs. Unduly simplifying or systematic speculation as to when Swift is talking and when his "persona," or about their "diametrically opposite" meanings if both are talking at once, often turns masks into persons, and induces in some critics the most absurd expectations of coherently developed characterisation. Thus W. B. Ewald's classic work on *The Masks of Jonathan Swift* footnotes its discussion of the fools-knaves passage with the astonishing statement that "The author's interest in observing and performing anatomical dissections is a characteristic which remains undeveloped in the *Tale* and which does not fit very convincingly the sort of *persona* Swift has set up" (though there actually *is*, if one wants it, "consistency" in the fact that the "author" is the sort of fool who performs experiments to discover the obvious!).

It is, of course, true that the "author" uses "fool" as a term of praise, as Cibber in the *Dunciad* praises Dulness. The Digression on Madness is a "praise of folly," and the "author" proudly declares himself "a Person, whose Imaginations are hard-mouth'd, and exceedingly disposed to run away with his *Reason*." The *Tale* presents, in its way, quite as much of an upside-down world as Pope's poem, but relies much less systematically on any single or dominant *verbal* formula. I do not mean that the *Dunciad* lacks that rudimentary two-way traffic between terms of praise and blame which we see in the *Tale* when, for example, the "author" praises his "Fool" as "a Man truly wise," although it may be true that even at this level the *Tale*'s ironic postures are more teasingly unstable (indeed the "author" seems not only to be scrambling simple valuations of wisdom and folly, but also perverting the "true" paradox that "folly is wisdom"). But the poem's mock-exaltation of fools rests essentially on a few strongly signposted terms (*dunce, dull*, etc.), which advertise the main ironic formula, and guarantee its fundamental predictability. When we feel uneasy or embarrassed in the *Dunciad*, it is because the main irony is *too* consistently sustained, rather than not enough. When Cibber praises Dulness ("whose good old cause I yet defend," "O! ever gracious . . . ," I.165,173, etc.), we may feel that Pope's blame-by-praise becomes awkward, not because the formula threatens to slip, but because it strains belief through overdoing. The implausibility may be no greater in itself than the hack's celebration of "Serene Peaceful States." But Cibber's praise has the slow unemphatic stateliness of a rooted conviction, while the hack's occurs in a context full of redirections, "Fool" being disturbed by "Knaves," as indeed the paragraph's happy style is disturbed throughout by alien intensities (flayed woman, beau's innards). Cibber at such moments fails to take off into the freer air of Pope's satiric fantasy, and solidifies instead into an improbably oversimplified "character." His heavy consistency embarrasses differently from the "inconsistencies" of Swift's hack, who, being in a sense no character at all, obeys no laws but those of his creator's anarchic inventiveness. The embarrassments in Pope are rare, but damaging. They are unintended, and disturb that poise and certainty of tone essential to Pope's verse. In Swift's satiric ambience, embarrassment is radical: it is a moral rather than an aesthetic thing, and is the due response to the rough edges and subversions of a style whose whole nature it is to undermine certainties, including the certainties it consciously proclaims.

Such blurred and shocking interchange (rather than sharp ironic opposition) between speaker and satirist is not confined to unruly works like the *Tale*. It occurs even in the *Modest Proposal*, that most astringent and tautly formulaic of Swift's writings. When the proposer uses the famous phrase, "a Child, *just dropt*

from its Dam," a shock occurs because the style has hitherto given no unmis-
takeable indication of its potential nastiness. Swift means the phrase to erupt in
all its cruel violence, yet it is formally spoken by the proposer, and we are not to
suppose *him* to be a violent, or an unkind, man. Is the nasty phrase "inconsistent"
with his character? In a way, yes. On the other hand, part of Swift's irony is that
prevailing values are so inhumane, that a gentle and moderate man will take all
the horror for granted. If he can sincerely assert his humanity while advocating
monstrous schemes, may he not also be expected to use a nasty phrase calmly
and innocently? In which case, the usage might be "consistent" with his character, thus indicating "diametrical" opposition between him and Swift. But inhumane propaganda which claims, or believes itself, to be humane (say that of a
"sincere" defender of apartheid), does not use inhumane language; and we should
have to imagine the speaker as incredibly insensitive to English usage, if he really
wanted himself and his scheme to seem as humane as he believed they were.
Such discussion of the "character" and his "consistency" leads to deserts of circu-
larity. But the problem hardly poses itself in the reading (as it poses itself, down
to the question of insensitivity to usage, over Cibber's praise of Dulness), and
what becomes apparent is the irrelevance, rather than the truth or untruth, of the
terms. The violent phrase is not an "inconsistency" but a dislocation, among
other dislocations. It has nothing to say about character, but breaks up a formula
(the formula of a calm, kindly advocacy of horrible deeds), within a style which
both includes such formulas and is given to breaking them up. Thus, when (in
contrast to the *Dunciad's* blame-by-praise, where it is easy to translate one set of
terms into its opposite) Swift's speakers praise fools, or proclaim their humanity
in brutal language, our reaction is to oscillate nervously between speaker and
satirist. If we bring this oscillation into the open by asking (as critics are always
asking) whether a bad speaker is using bad terms in a good sense, or whether
Swift himself is making some form of explosive intervention, we find no meaningful answer. But there is a sense in which it is a meaningful *question*, for it
brings into the open an uncertainty which is essential to the style.

The uncertainty is most strikingly illustrated in the Digression's "Knaves."
For it is this electrifying term, with all its appearance of simplifying finality,
which most resists tidy-minded schematisms of parallel-and-opposite valuation,
and the rest. If "Fool" was good to the "author" and bad to Swift, are "Knaves"
bad to the "author" and good to Swift? Does the sentence's impact really reside
in our feeling that "Knave" is the fool's word for a quality Swift would name
more pleasantly? If so, which quality? The answer is deliberately indistinct. Perhaps the "Knaves" are those "Betters" who, in the Preface to the *Battle of the
Books*, are said to threaten the serenity of fools (the Preface too is "of the Author,"
though an "author" at that moment more similar than opposite to Swift). But if

this points to a partial explanation, it does so *ex post facto*, and is not experienced in the reading. To the extent that we are, in context, permitted to escape the suggestion that the world is absolutely divided into fools and knaves, we confront alternatives that are elusive, unclear. If we do not take "Knaves" as Swift's word, literally meant, we cannot simply dismiss it as coming from the "author" and to be therefore translatable into something less damaging. We cannot be sure of the nature of any saving alternative, and may even uneasily suspect that we are in a fool's "Serene Peaceful State" for imagining that such alternatives exist. The style's aggressive indistinctness thus leaves damaging possibilities in the air, without pinning Swift down to an assertion definite enough to be open to rebuttal. And so it seems more appropriate to note the imprisoning rhetorical effect of "Fool among Knaves" than to determine too precisely who means what by those words. A rhetorical turn which wittily blocks off any respectable alternative to being a fool, is reinforced by those either-way uncertainties which the whole style induces in the reader. The reader is thus poised between the guilt of being merely human, and an exculpation which is as doubtful as the charges are unclear. The apparent definiteness of the epigram, and the reader's cloudy insecurity, mirror and complete each other in an overriding effect of impasse.

Fools and knaves go proverbially together, balancing one another in a variety of traditional sayings, a familiar source of more or less ready ironies for the witty phrase-maker. Swift's mot tends towards the most universalising of fool-knaves proverbs ("Knaves and fools divide the world"). But part of its flavour lies outside the grimmer implications, in the stylistic bravura which makes an established phrase complete itself in defiance of contextual expectations. The sudden appearance of "Knaves" at the end of the sentence has a delighted rightness. It is a witty and exhilarating idiomatic homecoming. The wit gives pleasure in itself, and playfully suggests the survival of linguistic order within a certain mental anarchy.

Wit (in the high as well as the restricted sense) knows its enemies well: "By *Fools* 'tis *hated*, and by *Knaves undone*" (*Essay on Criticism*, l. 507), and the erection of symmetries of style as a means of maintaining order among life's unruly energies is a familiar function of Augustan wit. Such symmetries have their effect more as acts of authorial presence, authorial defiances of chaos, than necessarily as embodiments of a widespread or active faith in stability or harmony. If the witty completeness of Swift's "Fool among Knaves" holds together a world of unruly energies, the joke is also, by its qualities of surprise and shock, an unruly energy in its own right. The idiomatic homecoming is achieved with such tear-away unpredictability, that it leaves equally open the possibility of a fresh engulfment in the hack author's chaos, or of further victorious but unexpected versatilities from the satirist. The sudden poise seems more like a tense individual triumph, uncertain to be repeated and wholly dependent on our momentarily vivid sense of the satirist's mastery, than like the revelation of a serenely ordered structure on which we may henceforth depend.

Even the more predictable symmetries of Augustan style, the parallelism, antithesis, balance, the patternings which complete a formula or satisfy an expectation (idiomatic, syntactical, metrical, or logical), do not always evoke harmonious parterres of order, stability and ease. Pope's couplets are full of the kind of symmetry in which damaging alternatives are so starkly paired as to suggest not the comforting boundaries of a fixed and ordered world, but closed systems of vice or unhappiness from which there is no apparent release. Many thumbnail characterisations in the *Epistle to a Lady*, for example, contain such imprisoning paradoxes as "A fool to Pleasure, and a slave to Fame," "The Pleasure miss'd her, and the Scandal hit," "Young without Lovers, old without a Friend" (ll. 62, 128, 246). These perhaps have a brevity of the ready-made, and certainly an external quality. Pope's concern is psychological, to define character, but his subjects here are either placed in predicaments mainly circumstantial ("Young without Lovers"), or described in very generalised psychological terms ("A fool to Pleasure") which suggest rapid and sketchy inference from outward behaviour. If the stylistic patterns evoke certain forms of impasse, rather than an easy sense of order, the impasse hardly becomes total or absolute. One is free to feel that circumstances might change or behaviour improve, whereas prisons of the mind will seem correspondingly inescapable because (as Milton's Satan discovered when he saw that hell was partly a mental state) they are carried everywhere within us. The typical impasse in Swift rests on a psychological factor, a perpetual perverse restlessness (madness close to badness) similar to what Johnson more compassionately saw as "that hunger of imagination which preys incessantly upon life" (*Rasselas*, XXX[I]: the fact that Satan's " 'my self am Hell,' " *Paradise Lost*, IV.75ff., is immediately followed by a "geographical" glimpse of bottomlessness, or infinite regression, "And in the lowest deep a lower deep / Still threatning to devour me," bears a suggestive relation to the endless coils of perverse self-complication of Swift's vision of man on earth, and to the ever-unsatisfied cravings of Johnson's passage). Such an impasse, especially in ages unused to the idea of a psychiatric "cure," is capable only of a religious solution, an annihilation of the self and its prisons within a greater imprisonment:

> Take mee to you, imprison mee, for I
> Except you 'enthrall mee, never shall be free.
> (Donne, "Batter my heart")

Swift and Johnson were not, like Milton's Satan, blocked off from the possibility of a saving "submission" ("that word / Disdain forbids me, and my dread of shame," *Paradise Lost*, IV.81–82), and both looked devoutly to "things eternal," but they normally thought of submission in less transcendent terms than those of Donne's prayer. They speak not of cures or liberations, but of disciplines and palliatives, of a super-imposition of moral solidities more practical than spiritually complete, of a concealment or silencing (not elimination) of doubts.

For Pope, such rescue operations seemed less necessary. His mental processes were less prone to residual discomfort, less likely than Swift's or Johnson's to abut in a subversive dissatisfaction. He could thus more readily accommodate them into a system complete and intricate enough to absorb inner subversiveness instead of crushing it. The *Essay on Man* imagines a world where there can ultimately be no imprisoning loose ends, because it holds all the answers: "All Discord, Harmony, not understood" (I.291). There is no sentimental denial of Discord, and Pope's satires give it due acknowledgment. But the world of the *Essay*, with its fresh, infectious delight in the conventional coherences of a theodicy, has no relevance for minds to whom Discord was a psychological condition rather than a philosophical problem, and neither Johnson nor Swift could have committed themselves to such a world, even as an imaginative abstraction or game. Johnson disliked the poem, but approved of the line "Man never Is, but always To be blest" (I.96). Johnson's comment is significant. It secularises and psychologises the line into meaning that no *present moment* can be happy, "but that, as every part of life, of which we are conscious, was at some point of time a period yet to come, in which felicity was expected, there was some happiness produced by hope" (Boswell, II.350–1: Hill-Powell aptly gloss this with Swift's "*perpetual Possession of being well Deceived*"). Pope's implication is very different. He is not so much concerned with the doomed unhappiness of present moments, as talking about an afterlife in which the devout and humble man may hope to find a happiness of whose nature he at present remains ignorant. The emphasis of Pope's preceding line, "Hope springs eternal in the human breast," is expansive and positive, not tiredly cynical in the way popular quotation often assumes, nor "realistically" earthbound in Johnson's way. For in Johnson's reading, hope becomes a useful if necessarily delusive alleviation, not cure, of an incurable human dissatisfaction. Like alcohol: pressed further as to whether "a man was not sometimes happy in the moment that was present, he answered, 'Never, but when he is drunk.' "

If those ordered stylistic dispositions characteristic of much Augustan writing can express, in Pope, states of vicious inextricability and impasse, the point is *a fortiori* true of Johnson, in both verse and prose: "wav'ring man . . . / Shuns fancied ills, or chases airy good"; "Human life is every where a state in which much is to be endured, and little to be enjoyed"; "Marriage has many pains, but celibacy has no pleasures"; "the more we enquire, the less we can resolve" (*Vanity*

of Human Wishes, ll. 7, 10; *Rasselas*, XI, XXVI). Such configurations are sometimes (in *Rasselas*) undercut by a mild humour, and we may often dissociate the
statements, in a formal sense, from the writer, who frequently does not speak in
his own person. Johnson, and Swift, differ from Pope in the kind and degree of
their authorial commitment to configurations of impasse. In Johnson, the commitment is most *direct* (not necessarily *closer* than Swift's, whose tense self-
involvement with his absurd and satirised speakers is extremely intimate, though
endlessly oblique; and whose subversive brilliance exists in a kind of mirror-
opposition to his hack's subversive folly). This is true even when he speaks through
fictional characters, for these often recognisably embody views, and styles of
thought and expression, also found in the more formally Johnsonian voices of
the *Rambler* or the conversations in Boswell's *Life*. Johnson's wit is the most
subdued of the three writers', and the undercutting in *Rasselas* is mild, suggesting
not dissociation but a ruefully avuncular endorsement. Johnson's eloquent liter-
alness, and the emphasis which he places on the psychological factor in the human condition, contribute an impression of laboured introspective involvement
far removed from the confident externalised precisions of Pope. Certain twists
and countertwists of the human mind, which Swift renders through feats of ironic
mimicry, Johnson can *state* with an astonishing and compassionate baldness:

> Then say how hope and fear, desire and hate,
> O'erspread with snares the clouded maze of fate,
> Where wav'ring man, betray'd by vent'rous pride,
> To tread the dreary paths without a guide,
> As treach'rous phantoms in the mist delude,
> Shuns fancied ills, or chases airy good.
>
> *(Vanity,* ll. 5–10)

The last line does not confine itself to implying the vanity of man's pursuit of
good and avoidance of ills, but says that the good and ills on which his energies
are spent are themselves unreal, compulsively imaginary: the ironic completeness
of the human impasse, and its essentially *psychological* root, are simultaneously
made vivid.

The completeness, indeed, depends on the psychological nature, and Pope
is a good deal less emphatic on both points than either Johnson or Swift. Even
when his examples of mental imprisonment have relatively little tendency to shift
to a circumstantial or a behavioural plane, and instead dwell (as in the portrait
of Flavia) on a self-entrapped mental *constitution*:

> Wise Wretch! with Pleasures too refin'd to please,
> With too much Spirit to be e'er at ease,

> With too much Quickness ever to be taught,
> With too much Thinking to have common Thought:
> Who purchase Pain with all that Joy can give,
> And Die of nothing but a Rage to live,
>
> (*To a Lady*, ll. 95–100)

Pope is still, as in the other examples, offering what defines itself as an individual case. The poem's informing generalisations (" 'Most Women have no Characters at all,' " "Ladies, like variegated Tulips, show," "Woman's at best a Contradiction still," ll. 2, 41, 270) are so much window-dressing for the individual set-pieces. Unlike Johnson's individual "characters" in the *Vanity*, which are a long painful illustration of the opening lines, implicating the whole of mankind, Pope's have a buoyant autonomy which reduces the universalising frameworks to relative insignificance. If the portrait of Flavia is "general" and not merely "personal" satire (and it may indeed be "personal" in the most specific sense, as well as having wider applicability), it is general of the type, not comprehensive. Of the dozen-odd fool-knave passages listed in Abbott's *Concordance* of Pope, not one has the globally imprisoning reach of Swift's mot. When, indeed, a Popeian character seeks to involve large sections of mankind into one or other of the two alternatives (Sir Gilbert, who "holds it for a rule, / That 'every man in want is knave or fool' " in *Epistle to Bathurst*, ll. 103–4, or Atossa, who

> Shines, in exposing Knaves, and painting Fools,
> Yet is, whate'er she hates and ridicules,

in *To a Lady*, ll. 119–20), it is on the slanderer and not his many victims that Pope lets the trap fall. Such firm delimiting of the attack permits a confident self-exclusion for both poet and reader. Pope is more cleanly dissociated than either Swift or Johnson from his speakers and characters, not only in upside-down works like the *Dunciad*, but (thanks to formalised rhetorical postures) even when the damaging statements are *spoken* not by the characters, but by the poet about them. Swift's wider and more damaging comprehensiveness implicates both himself and his reader, and permits neither to stand outside; in this way, as well as through the tense intimacies of the style, Swift's satire is so general that it becomes personal—and of the second and first, not only of the third, person.

The buoyancy of Pope's categorisations may be due to an active feeling that there exist, not just saving possibilities but actual worlds of order and decency, outside them. But there is certainly a quite individual delight in creating little fictions of order around cases of inconsistency and contradiction. The lines in which Flavia becomes immured within her own self-contradictions convey the poet's systematising triumph more strongly than they oppress us with her impasse.

His rhetoric here, as in other places, very strongly advertises its dominating stabilities. Each finality, each climax, even each shocking anticlimax, take their place in a well signposted pattern which is actually *style-induced*. There may be startling reversals, but they are always part of a visible rhythm of rising and falling, inflation and bathos, deception and undeception, and there is nothing which erupts in such sudden defiance of all expectation or pattern as Swift's "Fool among Knaves." "Inconsistency" yields special satisfactions, not (as in Swift) of mimicry, but of organisation. Hence not only the crisp buoyancies of single-line epigrams, but the relaxed, lingering amplitude, the easy metrical sweep that savours itself as it prepares sudden quickenings to conclusiveness, of such lines as these:

> Rufa, whose eye quick-glancing o'er the Park,
> Attracts each light gay meteor of a Spark,
> Agrees as ill with Rufa studying Locke,
> As Sappho's diamonds with her dirty smock.
>   (*To a Lady*, ll. 21–24)

Whenever "Order in Variety we see" (*Windsor Forest*, l. 15), it is less the "universal harmony" that we sense, than the creative delight of the poet in inventing it: even the *real* landscape in *Windsor Forest* to which the words refer seems (if the word may be imagined in a favourable sense) "staged." And those generalisations which impute a widespread and disreputable human variousness, may oddly carry more pleasure than pain. Pope's couplet about women being like the "variegated Tulips" (*To a Lady*, ll. 41–42) is itself ironic, and prefaces some accounts of strange and perverse states, but there is a pleasure, turning to gallantry, in the image's momentary power to systematise, so that a combined elegance, in the women and in Pope's ordering of their variety, survives the sarcasm: "Tis to their Changes that their charms they owe." Contrast the ending of *The Lady's Dressing Room*, where Swift combines women, tulips and ideas of order: "Such Order from Confusion sprung, / Such gaudy Tulips rais'd from Dung."

But Pope's usual way with damaging generalisations is to turn quickly to particulars, which are more amendable to the sort of enclosed definition which lets the rest of humanity out. "Characters" overwhelm their universalising context. In the *Epistle to Cobham*, the generalising lip service to human nature's "puzzling Contraries" (l. 124) is even greater than in *To a Lady*: "Our depths who fathoms, or our shallows finds, / Quick whirls, and shifting eddies, of our minds?" (ll. 29–30). The corresponding stress on triumphs of individual categorisation is also greater. The "ruling passion" seems a convenient formula less because it is a particularly good means to psychological insights than because of the pleasures of conclusive definition which is yields:

> Search then the Ruling Passion: There, alone,
> The Wild are constant, and the Cunning known.
>   (ll. 174ff.)

The satisfactions are largely aesthetic. The lengthy portrait of Wharton which follows this couplet is full of vivid debating triumphs:

> This clue once found, unravels all the rest,
> The prospect clears, and Wharton stands confest.
> . . . .
> Ask you why Wharton broke thro' ev'ry rule?
> 'Twas all for fear the Knaves should call him Fool.
>   Nature well known, no prodigies remain,
> Comets are regular, and Wharton plain.

If the concept of a "ruling passion" is something whose dialectical completeness imprisons the satiric victim, and if Pope's play of paradox and antithesis reinforces this imprisonment, there is nevertheless in the poem a feeling not of imprisonment but of release. "The prospect clears": such manifest delights of the controlling intellect have at least as much vitality as the turpitudes of Wharton and the rest. Contrast the very different finality of Swift's famous mot about Wharton's father, where the witty energy is entirely devoted to closing-in on the victim, and where the astringency of the prose-rhythms makes Pope's verse seem almost jaunty:

> He is a Presbyterian in Politics, and an Atheist in Religion; but he chuseth at present to whore with a Papist.

This astringency is revealing. It is often found where Swift practises what we may call couplet-rhetoric, that style in both verse and prose whose qualities of balance, antithesis, and pointedness mirror (ironically or not) Augustan ideals of coherence, regularity and decorous interchange, as well as paradoxes of enclosed self-contradiction. He seldom wrote heroic couplets, perhaps resisting the almost institutionalised sense of order which the form seemingly aspires to proclaim, and preferring more informal verse styles. His more exuberant effects, unlike Pope's, occur in more open-ended or unpredictable styles, and the patternings of a pointed or epigrammatic manner frequently freeze in his hands to a slow harsh deliberateness. The fact that such patternings occur mostly in his prose may have something to do with the greater amplitude of the medium, which makes possible longer, slower units of sense. But there is no Popeian buoyancy in Johnson's verse, and plenty in Fielding's prose, as the following passage shows:

Master Blifil fell very short of his companion in the amiable quality of
mercy; but as he greatly exceeded him in one of a much higher kind,
namely, in justice: in which he followed both the precepts and example of Thwackum and Square; for though they would both make
frequent use of the word mercy, yet it was plain that in reality Square
held it to be inconsistent with the rule of right; and Thwackum was
for doing justice, and leaving mercy to Heaven. The two gentlemen
did indeed somewhat differ in opinion concerning the objects of this
sublime virtue; by which Thwackum would probably have destroyed
one half of mankind, and Square the other half.

(*Tom Jones*, III.x)

This may recall some of the passages from Pope's *Epistle to a Lady*: balance,
contrast, a tremendous display of powers of summation, an obvious delight in
the feats of style which so memorably and satisfyingly categorise some unsavoury
facts. There is, too, the confident authorial presence, a decorous and gentlemanly
self-projection, simplified but enormously alive, free of the vulnerabilities of undue intimacy with the reader or undue closeness to the material, yet proclaiming
an assured and reassuring moral control. The categorisations point to a kind of
vicious closed system, but unlike Swift's imprisoning paradoxes and like those of
Pope, they deal with single persons or types, rather than with mankind or at least
with wide and damagingly undefined portions of it. Moreover, the kind of exuberance found in Fielding as in Pope turns the closed systems into authorial triumphs of definition, instead of allowing them to generate an oppressive feeling
of impasse. When Swift is exuberant on Fielding's or Pope's scale, he does not
produce a finality towards which the preceding rhetoric has been visibly tending,
but assaults us with sudden shocks of *re*definition, turning us into knaves if we
refuse to be fools. Fielding, like Pope, rounds his paradoxes to a conclusiveness
which, being both prepared-for and specific, limits their applicability and creates
a feeling of release. If the buoyant brevities of Pope's couplets are absent in
Fielding's passage, the amplitude of the prose medium in his case permits versatilities of elaboration, of weaving and interweaving, which are their counterpart
in exuberant definition.

Prose, then, does not in itself make couplet-rhetoric astringent. Here, however, is Gulliver on prime ministers:

he never tells a *Truth*, but with an Intent that you should take it for a
Lye; nor a *Lye*, but with a Design that you should take it for a *Truth*.

(*GT*, IV.vi)

and on the causes of war:

Sometimes one Prince quarrelleth with another, for fear the other should quarrel with him. Sometimes a War is entered upon, because the Enemy is too *strong*, and sometimes because he is too *weak*. Sometimes our Neighbours *want* the *Things* which we *have*, or *have* the Things which we want

(*GT*, IV.v)

These passages create little "anti-systems," absurdly self-consistent worlds of perverse motivation, whose complete disconnection from humane and rational purposes gives them an air of unreality, of disembodied vacancy. (The vision is partly a satiric counterpart to Johnson's tragic sense of man, shunning "fancied ills" and chasing "airy good.") Such satiric systematisations are not uncommon in Augustan literature, and Pope's *Moral Essays* also occasionally turn excesses of vice and irrationality into paradoxical pseudo-systems. Pope does not, however, allow them to take on so much crazy autonomy, but often refers them to an all-embracing ruling passion. Because Swift deliberately withholds explanations at this level, we have to fall back on some absolute notion of the ingrained perversity of the human species, which alone can account for such ghoulishly self-sustaining perversity.

Above all, where the epigrammatic summations of Pope or Fielding suggest that vicious matters have been "placed" or disposed of, there is here a sense of being weighed down. The categorisations are witty and precise, but the voice is flat and rasping, not buoyant with those righteous energies with which Pope and Fielding can outmatch the most viciously animated turpitudes. I suggest that this astringency is Swift's rather than Gulliver's, so far as we bother to disentangle them. This is not (once again) to say that Gulliver and Swift are identical, but that the feeling seems to come from behind the Gulliver who is speaking. Within a page of the last passage, in the same conversation or series of conversations, Gulliver gives this, not astringent but high-spirited, account of human war:

I could not forbear shaking my Head and smiling a little at his Ignorance. And, being no Stranger to the Art of War, I gave him a Description of Cannons, Culverins, Muskets, Carabines, Pistols, Bullets, Powder, Swords, Bayonets, Sieges, Retreats, Attacks, Undermines, Countermines, Bombardments, Seafights; Ships sunk with a Thousand Men; twenty Thousand killed on each Side; dying Groans, Limbs flying in the Air: Smoak, Noise, Confusion, trampling to Death under Horses Feet: Flight, Pursuit, Victory; Fields strewed with Carcases left for Food to Dogs, and Wolves, and Birds of Prey; Plundering, Stripping, Ravishing, Burning and Destroying. And, to set forth the Valour of my own dear Countrymen, I assured him,

that I had seen them blow up a Hundred Enemies at once in a Siege,
and as many in a Ship; and beheld the dead Bodies drop down in
Pieces from the Clouds, to the great Diversion of all the Spectators.

(*GT*, IV.v)

The note of animated pleasure is at odds with the preceding astringency, and
with the notion (see especially the *later* stress on this, IV.vii) that he was in these
conversations already disenchanted with humanity: but there is a very similar,
complacently delighted, account of war given to the King of Brobdingnag before
Gulliver's disenchantment (II.vii). The method of the *Travels*, putatively written
after the disenchantment, is often to have Gulliver present himself partly as he
was at the relevant moment in the past, and not merely as he might now see
himself, so that in both chapters (II.vii and IV.v) twin-notes of affection and
dislike might be felt to mingle or alternate. Unless we are prepared to regard
Gulliver as a very sophisticated ironist or rhetorician (let alone a highly developed
Jamesian consciousness) — and some readers are — we must feel that the alterna-
tions are modulations of Swift's ironic voice. Even if we deny Gulliver's pleasure
in the list about war, we cannot deny the list's comic exuberance, and its difference from the dry epigrams of a moment before. However we describe Gulliver's
attitude at this time, the shift cannot be attributed to any significant variation in
his feelings, just as the inordinate and chaotic cataloguing cannot be accounted
for as a subtly motivated departure from Gulliver's earlier announcement in IV.v
that he is only reporting "the Substance" (and an ordered summary at that) of
these conversations. The modulations in the *actual* atmosphere as we read em-
phasise again the abstractness of any separation of Swift from his speaker (even
where that speaker, unlike the *Tales*', has a name, wife, family and other tokens
of identity). Swift's most expansive satiric energies kindle not at those sharp and
witty summations which would have delighted Fielding or Pope, but at the
humour of Gulliver's anarchic submission to an evil whose chaotic vitality has
not been subdued to epigrammatic definition. At the mental level at which we,
as readers, respond to such transitions, we are face to face with Swift's inner
fluctuations, without intermediaries. Big men, little men, Gulliver and the rational
horses, become so many circus animals, deserting. The encounter is, of course,
unofficial: we do not admit it to ourselves, as distinct from experiencing it, and
no suggestion arises of Swift's conscious design. When Swift participates harshly
in Gulliver's tart epigrams there is no formal difficulty in imagining that the two
converge, almost *officially*. But when the tartness unpredictably gives way to
Gulliver's unruly exuberance (whether Gulliver is felt *at that instant* to hate war
or to relish it is not a problem which occurs to us in the reading, as distinct from
knowing Swift hates it, and sensing the exuberance), Swift's participation is un-

official and closer, a variant form of that mirror-relationship I have already suggested between an unruly and right-minded Swift who wrote the *Tale*, and the
Tale's unruly but mad and wicked "author."

These identities establish themselves in that very charged penumbra where
the satirist's personality overwhelms his own fictions, in a huge self-consciousness.
It is no coincidence, from this point of view, that Swift's *Tale* is both a pre-
enactment and an advance parody of Sterne; nor that the self-irony, at once self-
mocking and self-displaying, of Sterne, or Byron, or Norman Mailer (whose
Advertisements for Myself, for example, use every trick that the *Tale* satirically
*ab*used, digressions, self-interruptions and solipsisms, solipsistic reminders of digression or solipsism, etc.) sometimes develops from Swift or shares formal elements with his work. The major formal difference is that Swift's "authors" (the
hack, the proposer, Gulliver) are predominantly satirised figures, officially Swift's
complete antithesis most of the time, whereas the speakers or narrators of the later
writers are either identical with their creators (as in many of Mailer's *Advertisements*), or projections and facets, hardly massively dissociated. The satiric plots
and formulae which guarantee this dissociation in Swift may be thought of as
immense protective assertions of the Super-Ego, part of the same process which
sees to it that potentially "gratuitous" effects of any length are in fact more or
less subdued within frameworks of moral allegory. Because Swift's person is not
openly permitted to take the slightest part in the affair, his self-mockery (for example) is denied all the luxuries of coy self-analysis available to the later writers.
(Where he does, however, speak through voices which are direct self-projections,
as in *Cadenus and Vanessa* or the *Verses on the Death*, a tendency to such luxuries
becomes evident.) The fact that Swift's presence remains felt despite the formal
self-dissociation creates between the reader and Swift an either/or relation whose
very indefiniteness entails more, not less, intimacy. In that whirlpool of indefiniteness, where any tendency to categorise is arrested, individual characters become
fluid and indefinite, as in Sterne, despite the un-Sterne-like (but rather nominal
and cardboard) firmness of "characters" like the modest proposer, or like Gulliver
in his more self-consistent interludes. There is a relation between this and Swift's
readiness in some moods to think of the human mind as prone to bottomless
spirals of self-complication. An implication that hovers over both is that human
behaviour is too unpredictable to be usefully classified in rounded conceptions of
"personality," as "in (or out of) character." Despite its strong moral point of
reference, Swift's self-implicating sense of our anarchic tortuosity is close in conception to some of those visions of complexity which in our time are often em-
bodied in the extraordinarily recurrent image of a spiral (and its relations, vortex,
whirlpool, winding stair, endless ladder, vicious circle), with all its suggestions
of perpetual movement and interpenetrating flux. We think of the Yeats of *Blood*

and the Moon, who charged the image with a direct and passionate self-commitment, and with splendours and miseries which Swift would shrink from as too grandiloquent,

> I declare this tower is my symbol; I declare
> This winding, gyring, spiring treadmill of a stair is my ancestral stair;
> That Goldsmith and the Dean, Berkeley and Burke have travelled
>   there.
> Swift beating on his breast in sibylline frenzy blind
> Because the heart in his blood-sodden breast had dragged him down
>   into mankind,

but whose inclusion of Swift represents no mean insight; of "those endless stairs from the buried gaming rooms of the unconscious to the tower of the brain" in Mailer; of the dialectical psychologies of Sartre or R. D. Laing.

A reflection of this on a more or less conscious, or "rhetorical," plane are those familiar fluidities of style: the irony seldom docile to any simple (upside-down or other) scheme; "masks" and allegories seldom operating in an unruffled point by point correspondence with their straight nonfictional message, or with sustained consistency to their own fictional selves; stylistic procedures at odds with one another, or deliberately out of focus with the main feeling of the narrative; contradictory implications on matters of substance. The effect is to preclude the comforts of definiteness, while blocking off retreats into woolly evasion, so that both the pleasures of knowing where one stands, and those of a vagueness which might tell us that we need not know, are denied.

Pope's writing, by contrast, depends on a decorous clarity of relationship (with the reader and subject), without the active and radical ambiguity we find in Swift. Pope's speakers (outside the *Dunciad*) are usually not enemies, from whom he must signpost his dissociation, but rhetorically simplified projections of himself (as urbane Horatian commentator, righteously angry satirist, proud priest of the muses). The somewhat depersonalised postures are traditional and "public," secure within their rhetorical traditions (and so not subject to unpredictable immediacies), and they permit certain grandeurs of self-expression precisely because the more intimate self recedes from view. Urbane or passionate hauteurs ("Scriblers or Peers, alike are *Mob* to me," "I must be proud to see / Men not afraid of God, afraid of me") can then occur without opening the poet to easy charges of crude vanity. The "masks" of Pope may thus be thought of as melting the poet's personality in a conventional or public role, but also as a release for certain acts of authorial presence. The finalities of the couplet form serve Pope in a similar way. They formally sanction a degree of definiteness which might otherwise seem open to charges of arrogance or glibness. The clearly patterned artifice hardly engulfs Pope. He moves within it with so much vitality and such an assurance of colloquial rhythm, that a powerfully dominating presence is always felt. But it remains a simplified presence, and Swift is in many ways paradoxically closer to his parodied enemies than is Pope to his own rhetorical selves.

But if couplets help Pope to formalise his presence, and to free it from certain inhibiting vulnerabilities, the effect is largely personal to Pope, and not primarily a cultural property of the form. Couplets do not, in Johnson, guarantee to suppress vulnerability, nor create triumphs of self-confidence; and their prose-counterparts do not in Swift (as they do in Fielding) attenuate the close intimacy of the satirist's presence. The balanced orderliness of couplet-rhetoric need not, even in Pope, reflect a serenity of outlook, nor a civilisation which is confident, stable and in harmony with itself. The *Dunciad*, like the *Tale* and *Gulliver*, envisages cherished ideals not only under threat, but actually collapsing. The absurd moral universes which are locked away in the neat satiric patternings of both Swift and Pope often show "order" parodying itself in its nasty uncreative antithesis. Each vicious "anti-system" seems the ironic expression not of an Augustan order, but of a "rage for order" gone sour. Pope's later style (at least) suggests no easy dependence on stabilities visibly and publicly achieved, but (like Swift's) highly personal encroachments on chaos.

Pope's way with chaos, however, is to keep his distance. He is temperamentally one of those for whom categorisation and wit offer satisfactions which as such reduce chaos, or keep it at bay: not only aesthetic satisfactions as, once labelled by "ruling passions," the "prospect clears," but the comforting moral solidity of a decisive summation, however damaging or pessimistic. A style had to be forged for this, since the enemy to be mastered was subtle and resilient enough to expose the smallest verbal evasion or complacency. Pope's rhetoric suggests not denial but *containment* of powerful and subtle forces, and thrives on an excited decisiveness. If his lapses lead to complacency and patness, his strengths are those of a thrilling and masterful vision, in which delicate perceptions and massive urgencies of feeling marvellously cohere. Swift's rhetoric is no less masterful, but its whole nature is to suggest forces which cannot be contained, thus tending away from categorisation. This is often evident at moments of clinching finality, and nowhere more clearly than in the phrase about the "Fool among Knaves." The clear and uncompromising lines of the completed epigram imply, as we saw, that "knaves and fools divide the world." But the surprise of this implication, its violation of the general run of the preceding argument, and our impulse to discount something (we do not know what, nor how much) because the words are formally spoken by the mad "author" cause a blur of uncertainty to play over the cheeky patness of the phraseology. Categorisation yields to unresolved doubts. The clinching phrase, subverting its own finality, becomes disorderly and inconclusive. If it is also a self-assertion, buoyant with the satirist's masterful grasp over his material, it is not, in Pope's manner, part of a steady rhetoric of definition, but seems a dazzling momentary victory wrested from chaos. Of course, the playing for sudden dazzling victories, and to some extent the chaos itself, are also a rhetoric, though not (like Pope's) self-announced and openly visible as such. It is important to Pope's manner that he should seem to stand clear-sightedly on top of his material; and essential to Swift's to appear, as the phrase from *Lord Jim* puts it, in the destructive element immersed.

This is evident not merely in the mechanics of verbal style, narrowly conceived. Whole allegorical sequences, whose straightforward message has Swift's full endorsement, dissolve in a self-undercutting inconsistency, or explode in violence. The most unsettling thing about the Academy of Lagado, and especially its School of Political Projectors, is not the allegorical *substance*, but the Swiftian manoeuvres which force change of focus in the midst of an apparent moral certainty. The projectors are associated not only with predictably silly and repugnant programmes, but, by an astonishing redirection in III.vi, also with "good" schemes ("of teaching Ministers to consult the publick Good," etc.), some of which in turn dissolve into an Ubu-like absurdity (like the zanily beneficent "cruelty" of eliminating political dissension by a redistribution of the mixed brains of opponents, lobotomised in couples for the purpose), and thence back to crude totalitarian horrors. Or consider this initially straightforward allegory from section IV of the *Tale*:

> whoever went to take him by the Hand in the way of Salutation, *Peter* with much Grace, like a well educated Spaniel, would present them with his *Foot*.

This is one of several Swiftian jokes about the papal ceremony, and the passage so far is adequately accounted for in Wotton's gloss, which Swift prints in a note: "*Neither does his arrogant way of requiring men to kiss his Slipper, escape Reflexion*." The passage then continues:

> and if they refused his Civility, then he would raise it as high as their Chops, and give them a damn'd Kick on the Mouth, which hath ever since been call'd a *Salute*.

This development is outside the scope of Wotton's comment, outside the clean outlines of the allegory. It is not, as with the school of projectors, a redirection of the allegory, but an overspilling. One may argue it into the allegorical scheme by saying (accurately enough) that it represents the authoritarian brutality of the Roman Church. But the real force of the passage is to explode the emphasis away from the domain of allegorical correspondence as such.

The sudden violence is only one of several means of subversion, capping other subversions inherent in the context. Swift's appropriation, here and throughout the *Tale*, of Wotton's hostile exegesis, is not merely a means of explaining the allegory. Various piquancies of attack and of mocking self-exhibition, which lie outside the mere purposes of allegorical translation, are at work: the bravura of exploiting an enemy's attack for the serious illumination of one's own work; the tendency of this trick, while explaining the text, to mock it as requiring such solemn annotation, and from such a source; all the conventional seasoning of mock-scholarship, and so on. These effects combine with the fact that the allegory, like everything else, is spoken by the crazy "author," and that it is an allegory which parodies allegories. The straightforward import of the story of the three brothers is thus not only undercut, but fragmented by a host of competing energies. Swift's real commitment to the direct import or core (the potted history of the Church) and to the primary satiric implications (the "Abuses in Religion") becomes complicated by huge and distracting pressures: of self-mockery, of self-concealment, of tortuous and exuberant self-display. To say that this self-mockery simply subverts to the allegory, or satirises allegories in general, would be too crude, not only because part of the allegory somehow survives straight, but also because that diffusive spikiness injected by Swift is an attacking thing, *adding* to the satire's total fund of aggression and reinforcing the allegory's attack by that fact. But there is certainly, in practice, an exposure of the limits of the allegory to express all that Swift wants, to a degree which far exceeds the superficial and routine self-deflations of "self-conscious narrative."

The centre cannot hold. These unharnessed centrifugal energies of the form, its huge disruptive egotism, mirror the satirist's conscious vision of man's self-absorbed mental restlessness endlessly spiralling away from the rule of sense and virtue. The satirist is reflected in that mirror, "satirised" beyond all his rhetorical reaches, yet *aptly* implicated, since his attack, so deeply rooted (as we saw) in a *psychological* diagnosis, extends to all mankind. Johnson was to take that vision a step away from moral censure, but largely by means of compassion and a rueful self-tolerance rather than by any radical reappraisal of moral standards. It is only much later that one hears of a "human condition," psychologically determined, but without God and without attribution of sin. Nevertheless, the vicious spirals, and those related energies (of sudden violence, or of deliquescence) which overspill their official (didactic or discursive) purposes, have the further point in common with black humour and the cult of the "gratuitous" that their world is no longer secure in its values. When straightforward categorisable vice has dissolved into the unpredictabilities of the *Tales'* freewheeling madness (the vice/madness equation is commonplace, but the *Tale* is surely something special), the most cherished finalities no longer seem to solve anything. A conclusiveness where, "Nature well known, no prodigies remain, / Comets are regular, and Wharton plain," yields to conclusions "where nothing is concluded." Swift and Johnson clung, of course, with an urgency often authoritarian and sometimes close to despair, to their faith in a traditional morality, to their Anglican piety and Augustan ideals of order. They had no consciously formulated sense that traditional values cannot any longer apply. This partly explains the tendency of Swift's "gratuitous" effects to dovetail into a moral argument, especially if they are protracted; and it doubtless has something to do with Swift's and Johnson's stylistic attachment to the perspicuous finalities of couplet-rhetoric, Swift's in some of his prose, Johnson's in prose and verse. But Johnson's laboured, eloquent sadness in this mode, and Swift's imprisoning harshness, also tell their story. So, I believe, does the corresponding tendency of Swift's prose to kindle to a ferocious vitality in proportion as (in much of the *Tale*, and in Gulliver's list about war) its subject grows anarchic. The radical difference from Pope lies here, for all Swift's conscious closeness to Pope's outlook, and for all the likelihood that he would have given Breton and the other modern theorists a most comfortless home in his *Tale*. The matter transcends official themes, and outward feelings, as it transcends mere couplets. Cultural disorder for cultural disorder, the Academy of Lagado's relatively lighthearted or low-pitched inconsequence (not to mention the *Tales'*) seems more disturbing than the *Dunciad*'s Fourth Book, Miltonic Darkness and all. This is perhaps part of what Leavis meant about Pope being more "positive" than Swift, and if so it leads me to an exactly opposite valuation of the two men. For if Pope's positives, even in defeat (when the massive heroic ruin of the *Dunciad* proclaims the world that has been lost), are vividly adequate to the crisis as Pope recreates it in all brilliant truthfulness, they do not measure up to the evoked quality of deepest malaise with which Swift *relives* that crisis. Swift's writing exists at a level where no act of containment, however complete and resourceful, can in the end be validated, its subject being, not Augustan culture, but the nature of man. And the matter of Swift's vitality in anarchic contexts is not wholly accounted for by Leavis's notion (in what is, despite its hostility, the most acute general discussion of Swift ever written) that Swift is most creatively alive in "rejection and negation." The slow harsh epigrams negate and reject just as much, and when it comes to Yahoos having "all the life," we may wonder whether (as in the *Tale*) Swift is not most profoundly in his element not merely as a scourge of anarchy, but as its *mimic*; participating inwardly, as well as protesting at those limitless escalations of folly and vice, those feverish spirals of self-complication. As the satire finally devolves from the third on to the first person, from world to gentle reader and back to the satirist, we could do worse than entertain the thought that Swift, in that place where all the ladders (and the spirals) start, was and sensed that he was, in all rebellious recalcitrance, himself Yahoo.

PATRICIA MEYER SPACKS

Some Reflections on Satire

The importance of the psychic disturbance satire creates is of course clearest and most significant in works of satiric intent. Jonathan Swift's *Modest Proposal for Preventing the Children of Ireland from being a Burden to their Parents or Country* demonstrates how effective a satiric device is the generation and complex maneuvering of the reader's uneasiness. Swift works, here as in his other satiric writing, by exploiting various degrees of awareness in his readers. One's responses to the *Modest Proposal* are likely to proceed by an orderly heightening and deepening of emotion. First the speaker presents himself as a rational, practical man. He invites our participation in his concern for Ireland, the concern of a man aware of economic realities but full of feeling as well: the first words of the piece are, "It is a melancholly Object . . ." We assume (I am trying to recapture the initial response to the essay: obviously a second or third reading contaminates the opening paragraphs with our knowledge of what is to come) — we assume that we are intended to identify with the speaker in his intent to make "these Children sound and useful Members of the Commonwealth," that the satiric target will be elsewhere. No uneasiness so far: everything seems set up to encourage our complacency at our ability to grasp social problems in larger and more meaningful terms than mere sentimentality.

We are not long allowed to remain in our state of self-satisfaction. The point at which we become suspicious of the speaker depends on the degree of our sensitivity. Is it at the end of the second paragraph, where his motivation seems connected with his desire to see his "Statue set up for a Preserver of the Nation"? Or in the fourth paragraph, where he refers to "a Child, *just dropt from its Dam*"? By the time we reach paragraph six, where the modest proposer

From *Genre* 1, no. 1 (January 1968), © 1967 by the Editors of *Genre*.

treats stealing as an economic solution with no apparent awareness of any moral question associated with it, we are almost certain to have become nervous; the next paragraph, with its consideration of boys and girls as salable commodities, is positively disturbing. The suggestion that children be sold for food occurs shortly thereafter, making further identification with the speaker finally untenable.

For a moment, then, we are turned adrift. As our skepticism about the speaker's values increases, we must question our own values, which have earlier seemed to coincide with his. The speaker, we begin to feel, is the object of satire; and we, as readers, are implicated. But the resultant uneasiness soon yields to a new kind of complacency. At least now we realize more than the speaker does; we can judge him with the superiority of moralists, recognize and condemn his moral impoverishment, shudder at the barbarity which Swift's diction constantly calls to our attention.

But we are not yet secure. The next series of disturbing suggestions concerns the state of affairs the proposer's suggestions are designed to correct. First the speaker claims that cruelty "hath always been with me the strongest Objection against any Project, how well soever intended." Apparently he does not find his own proposal cruel. Why not? Perhaps we answer that he lacks self-knowledge, he does not realize what he is suggesting. But he goes on to describe the people, "*dying*, and *rotting*, by *Cold* and *Famine*, and *Filth*, and *Vermin*"; to suggest that his proposal will have the advantage that "Men would become as *fond* of their Wives, during the Time of their Pregnancy, as they are now of their *Mares* in Foal, their *Cows* in Calf, or *Sows* when they are ready to farrow; nor offer to beat or kick them, (as is too *frequent* a Practice) for fear of a Miscarriage"; to reveal that at present the poorer tenants own nothing, "their Corn and Cattle being already seized, and *Money a Thing Unknown*." We begin to suspect what we only feel fully at the end of the essay: that the true horror is in the state of affairs that produces the proposal, not in the proposal itself, which comes to seem more and more dreadfully plausible. Is this cannibalism not, after all, quite rational; is it not, indeed, almost inevitable under the circumstances the projector so graphically and specifically describes? "I desire the Reader will observe," he writes, "that I calculate my Remedy *for this one individual Kingdom of Ireland, and for no other that ever was, is, or, I think, ever can be upon Earth*." He has looked coolly at the facts of the situation; sheer rationality has led him to his solution. Centuries of traditional morality forbid us to take it seriously; still we become aware of its compelling logic. Since we cannot accept the logic we recognize, we face a new dilemma, a more radical source of uneasiness: rationality itself is being called into question. If rational thinking leads to barbarity, must we reject our commitment to it? Does our contempt for the speaker involve us in contempt for clear-headedness? Is our regard for morality mere sentimentality, and misguided sentimentality at that?

Once more, Swift rescues us: we do not have to remain in our uneasiness, we climb to a new level of security and shift from satiric uneasiness (we are implicated, we can't even understand quite how, we don't know how to get out) to satiric superiority with the list of solutions which the proposer declares to be impossible because the Irish people will not put them into practice. These solutions supply a refreshing note of sanity (they are solutions which Swift straightforwardly recommended elsewhere). We grasp at them eagerly, and note that they combine economic awareness with moral sensitivity. Shopkeepers are to have "*a Spirit of Honesty, Industry, and Skill*"; at present they treat their customers unfairly. Absentees should be taxed, local production utilized, pride, vanity and idleness cured: throughout the long list, economic solutions merge with moral ones. We realize now that the proposer possesses rationality but not reason in the eighteenth-century definition, which makes reason a moral as well as a rational faculty (cf. the fourth book of *Gulliver's Travels*). We have new grounds for feeling superior to the projector who fails by Swift's clear standards, with which we now gratefully align ourselves. But Swift is not yet through with us.

A residue of uneasiness remains after the list of positive proposals because of the speaker's firm assurance that there is unlikely ever to be "some hearty and sincere Attempt to put *them in Practice*." The standard of true reason is tempting, we cling to the assurance it provides, but perhaps it is irrelevant to the immediate situation. The nature of that situation suddenly becomes more vivid, in the next to the last paragraph of the essay. The projector seems to recognize the possibility of objections to his proposal, but he challenges anyone to find a counter-proposal "equally innocent, cheap, easy, and effectual." Anyone who offers another solution, he points out, must consider two points:

> First, as Things now stand, how they will be able to find Food and Raiment, for a Hundred Thousand useless Mouths and Backs? And *Secondly*, There being a round Million of Creatures in human Figure, throughout this Kingdom; whose whole Subsistence, put into a common Stock, would leave them in Debt two Millions of Pounds *Sterling*; adding those, who are Beggars by Profession, to the Bulk of Farmers, Cottagers and Labourers, with their Wives and Children, who are Beggars in Effect; I desire those Politicians, who dislike my Overture, and may perhaps be so bold to attempt an Answer, that they will first ask the Parents of these Mortals, Whether they would not at this Day think it a great Happiness to have been sold for Food at a Year old, in the Manner I prescribe; and thereby have avoided such a perpetual Scene of Misfortunes, as they have since gone through; by the *Oppression of Landlords*; the Impossibility of paying Rent, without Money or Trade; the Want of common Sustenance, with

neither House nor Cloaths, to cover them from the Inclemencies of
the Weather; and the most inevitable Prospect of intailing the like, or
greater Miseries upon their Breed for ever.

This paragraph introduces no important new facts. With great economy
and point, it reviews data previously presented, and it suggests—almost enforces
—the cataclysmic shift of perspective hinted earlier. Through most of the essay
we have felt secure in our superiority to the projector. If we waver briefly in our
assurance about the grounds of our superiority, we proceed to the conviction that
by the highest standards we can judge him and find him wanting. Now, though,
his calm rationality suggests that he might with equal validity judge us and find
us wanting. The people he describes would think it a happiness to be sold for
food, to avoid the horrors of the life they live. The proposal that they be so sold is
barbarous; the situation that might lead the victims to welcome it is worse. Most
people, of course, accept the starvation, helplessness, hopelessness of masses of
others with perfect equanimity. The modest proposer has offered an intolerable
solution to an intolerable situation. We judge his solution inhuman, and condemn
him for suggesting it. But if the situation is worse than the solution, if it is even
equally bad, surely the people who accept it as the given state of affairs, who
coolly evaluate solutions and reject proposals and proposers alike without themselves doing anything to alleviate the problem—surely such people must be condemned. And who are they? The piece becomes an indictment of the people of
Ireland, who do nothing about their plight, and of the people of England, who
do nothing either; and, like so much of Swift's work, it reaches out beyond its
time and place to indict the twentieth-century reader who accepts as inevitable
man's inhumanity to man, who rests secure in his reason and morality without
involving himself in the horror of social inequity. Swift's positive standards include humanity as well as reason. If we take his essay seriously, allow ourselves
to be affected by it, we are left in a state of profound uneasiness, recognizing our
involvement in the evil to which we have earlier felt superior.

PETER STEELE

Terminal Days among the Houyhnhnms

A natural response to the last major episode of *Gulliver's Travels*, the "Voyage to the Houyhnhnms," might well include the sense of all but complete critical inadequacy. It is notorious, after all, that in much of Swift's best writing subtlety and simplicity go together: and if, accordingly, there are sections of his work to which one must sit lightly but firmly when attending, this fourth book, and in particular its last chapter, is a signal instance of the need for such a position. I think that this last chapter is the most masterly part of the whole of the *Travels*: and I propose here to examine some parts of it, in the hope of evoking certain features of the book as a whole.

The chapter begins with a passage which is strongly reminiscent of a number of others earlier in the work:

> THUS, gentle Reader, I have given thee a faithful History of my
> Travels for Sixteen years, and above Seven Months; wherein I have
> not been so studious of Ornament as of Truth. I could perhaps like
> others have astonished thee with strange improbable Tales; but I
> rather chose to relate plain Matter of Fact in the simplest Manner
> and Style; because my principal Design was to inform and not to
> amuse thee.

So it begins again—the quiet, enormous, persistent claim to be, at heart, one concerned with telling the truth, and concerned with nothing else. Behind it there echo similar claims: the publisher's, preeminently, at the beginning of the work: and Gulliver's fairly recent confession that "*Truth* appeared so amiable to me,

---

From *Southern Review* (Australia) 4, no. 3 (1971). © 1971 by the University of Adelaide.

that I determined upon sacrificing everything to it" (ch. 7). But for all the deliberative manner affected by Gulliver at various points in the *Travels*, he has often
been peculiarly inept at telling what might be called "the whole truth." This
ineptitude is no doubt bound up with his disposition to think that truth, while it
may be a costly thing to tell, is not complicated: that it requires at most a certain
amount of good faith, and about the same amount of attention to detail. With
these supposed present, he could in fact give "a faithful History of my Travels
for Sixteen Years, and above seven months" (ch. 12). An ironically inclined reader
might wonder whether any subsequent account would not be like the account
given by the mythical cabin boy on the voyage with the Ancient Mariner, who,
when asked what it had been like, said that at first there was a lot of ice, and
that afterwards they couldn't get enough to drink. It was true, but hardly the
truth of the voyage.

Gulliver's claim, though, goes well beyond a readiness to narrate what he
takes for the facts of the case. He is eloquent in his indignation against those
who pervert the truth. The indignation deepens and becomes more intriguing in
a long paragraph which begins,

> I COULD heartily wish a Law were enacted, that every Traveller,
> before he were permitted to publish his Voyages, should be obliged
> to make Oath before the *Lord High Chancellor*, that all he intended
> to print was absolutely true to the best of his Knowledge;

and concludes,

> But I forbear descanting further, and rather leave the judicious Reader
> to his own Remarks and Applications.
>
> (ch. 12)

The cardinal point in the paragraph is the sentence which goes,

> I imposed on myself as a Maxim, never to be swerved from, that I
> would *strictly adhere to Truth*; neither indeed can I be ever under
> the least Temptation to vary from it, while I retain in my Mind the
> Lectures and Examples of my noble Master, and the other illustrious
> *Houyhnhnms*, of whom I had so long the Honour to be an humble
> Hearer.
> —*Nec si miserum Fortuna Sinonem*
> *Finxit, vanum etiam, mendacemque improba finget.*

Now there are two elements in this which immediately give it away. The
first is the "neither . . . can I be ever under the least Temptation to vary from it,"
a claim which would be flatly incredible in any circumstances. The second is

what might be called the undertow in the quotation. The quotation comes from the point in the *Aeneid* at which Sinon, the professional trickster, is insinuating the Trojan Horse into Troy, and is claiming, as earnest of his good faith, that he will never play people false. Gulliver, taking the quotation at face value—as he takes virtually everything—is quite unaware that there is something peculiarly ironical in his appeal to the authority of the Houyhnhnms in the words used by Sinon to bring about acceptance of the Horse. He continues in this paragraph, as in what follows, to insist on the extent to which the Houyhnhnms are normative and ideal. One does not believe him here, and one never does in the "Voyage to the Houyhnhnms." It is not that he is not a painstaking observer; it is just that when he tries to be more than this, by bringing events into some kind of moral compass, he is at his most absurd.

Here as always, though, it would be an oversimplification to reduce Gulliver to the figure of a buffoon. In effect, to be Gulliver is not just to be the seamy side of man, or just to be the unknowing side of man. It is to be man perpetually falling away from being "achieved" man, and in that same act to be falling away from the consciousness of the terms of humanity. It is, in other words, in Swift's own mordant formula, to be not *animal rationale* but *rationis capax*, an ironic potentiality. Man being, in Swift's view, what he is, he can only be defined by contraries, negations, the characteristic shape of his failings.

The point may be made more decisively by considering the Houyhnhnms and the Yahoos. They have vexed many people in many ways: and the vexation has not always been of the sort Swift had in mind when he said that he wanted to "vex." The literature on these beings, particularly on the Houyhnhnms, is remarkable, and I do not intend to come to terms even with the substance of it here, beyond making a couple of points. It seems clear that Swift never meant anyone to choose between Houyhnhnms and Yahoos. In the work—their only environment, after all—they seem much more residual, dependent, even parasitic rhetorical entities than Gulliver himself is; and their true importance lies in their providing the opportunity for a series of encounters on his part. The fact, for instance, that the Houyhnhnms are clean, orderly, philosophical and quasi-aristocratic beings, and the Yahoos sordid, insatiable and servile, is no more an isolable datum in the *Travels* than the narrative structure is, or the presence of the sardonic catalogues. One makes what sense one can of any of these elements in terms of the whole: and by far the most important determining element in the work is Gulliver's ambiguous consciousness. It seems to me a mistaken move to take Houyhnhnms and Yahoos, even, as being *primarily* two kinds of parody of true humanity. If they are so, they are so mainly as objects of parodic choice on Gulliver's part. In the work as it is they are very important; but in their own right they are not only unimportant but unintelligible.

I think that the important thing, dramatically speaking, about the Houyhnhnms in the *Travels* is that Gulliver takes them to be an *absolute* authority. It
was under the instruction of the Houyhnhnm his master that, as he says, "*Truth*
appeared so amiable to me, that I determined upon sacrificing everything to it"
(ch. 7). There is something flatly idolatrous about a sacrifice of that kind: and
it is not surprising that Gulliver should conceive the purpose under the direction
of the Houyhnhnm. For he takes the Houyhnhnms to be not only impeccable
but also simply directive, unbending in either understanding or compassion, and
above all, unperplexed. Their real beauty in his eyes is not precisely their virtue
but the security of their virtue. Although they are largely indifferent to him (except for his "master," who is interested in remodelling him), and although Gulliver is subservient before them, there is really a kind of connivance, as he sees it,
between the purity of his purpose and views and the purity of their being. They
are his dream, the Yahoos his nightmare: but it is as if he has a unique right to
such a dream and such a nightmare. After all, as he says,

> I meddle not the least with any *Party*, but write without Passion,
> Prejudice, or Ill-will against any Man or Number of Men whatso-
> ever. I write for the noblest End, to inform and instruct Mankind,
> over whom I may, without Breach of Modesty, pretend to some
> Superiority, from the Advantages I received by conversing so long
> among the most accomplished *Houyhnhnms*.
>
> (ch. 12)

The modesty of that "some Superiority" disguises a little the claim to Apotheosis
—the claim that Gulliver is authentically "man" in a sense in which mankind in
general is not. It is, for all the deference, a demonic view of humanism; a view of
naked, effortless attainment of the state of *animal rationale*.

His appeal to the Houyhnhnm condition is an appeal to a similarly demonic
state. After mentioning the impropriety of invading the Lilliputians, the Brob-
dingagians or the Laputans, he considers the Houyhnhnms:

> Their Prudence, Unanimity, Unacquaintedness with Fear, and their
> Love of their Country would amply supply all Defects in the military
> Art. Imagine twenty Thousand of them breaking into the Midst of
> an *European* Army, confounding the Ranks, overturning the Car-
> riages, battering the Warriors' Faces into Mummy, by terrible yerks
> from their hinder Hoofs: For they would well deserve the Character
> given to Augustus; *Recalcitrat undique tutus*. But instead of Proposals
> for conquering that magnanimous Nation, I rather wish they were in a
> Capacity or Disposition to send a sufficient Number of their Inhabi-

tants for civilizing *Europe*; by teaching us the first Principles of Honour, Justice, Truth, Temperance, publick Spirit, Fortitude, Chastity, Friendship, Benevolence, and Fidelity. The *Names* of all which Virtues are still retained among us in most Languages, and are able to be met with in modern as well as ancient Authors; which I am able to assert from my own small Reading.

(ch. 12)

It is the ease of the transition from "battering the Warriors Faces into Mummy, by terrible Yerks from their hinder Hoofs" to "the first Principles of Honour, Justice, Truth" that is perhaps the most significant thing here. The Houyhnhnms are being proposed as an absolute power elite for whom physical violence of an apocalyptic kind is the easily imagined obverse of their habitual unearthly tranquility. Gulliver embraces both visions with equal ease, and counterposes only his claim about the absence of all virtue from England—a claim whose sarcastic force is trivial compared with what he has accepted.

This elitist preoccupation of Gulliver's is not peculiar to the last chapter of the book. It has been established and elaborated from much earlier on in the "Houyhnhnms." The power of a passage like this one is dependent in part upon the earlier collaboration between Gulliver and the Houyhnhnms, a collaboration which consists much less in his coming round to their opinions on one point or another than in his offering a reading of the world consonant with their intellectual titanism. Consider, for instance, the following passage:

SOMETIMES the Quarrel between two Princes is to decide which of them shall dispossess a Third of his Dominions, where neither of them pretend to any Right. Sometimes one Prince quarrelleth with another, for fear the other should quarrel with him. Sometimes a War is entered upon, because the Enemy is too *strong*, and sometimes because he is too *weak*. Sometimes our Neighbours *want* the *Things* which we *have*, or have the Things which we want; and we both fight, till they take ours or give us theirs. It is a very justifiable Cause of War to invade a Country after the People have been wasted by Famine, destroyed by Pestilence, or embroiled by Factions amongst themselves. It is justifiable to enter into a War against our nearest Ally, when one of his Towns lies convenient for us, or a Territory of Land, that would render our Dominions round and compact. If a Prince send Forces into a Nation, where the People are poor and ignorant, he may lawfully put half of them to Death, and make Slaves of the rest, in order to civilize and reduce them from their barbarous Way of Living. It is a very kingly, honourable, and frequent Practice,

when one Prince desires the Assistance of another to secure him
against an Invasion, that the Assistant, when he hath driven out the
Invader, should seize on the Dominions himself, and kill, imprison
or banish the Prince he came to relieve. Allyance by Blood or Marriage, is a sufficient Cause of War between Princes; and the nearer
the Kindred is, the greater is their Disposition to quarrel: *Poor* Nations
are *hungry*, and *rich* Nations are *proud*; and Pride and Hunger will
ever be at Variance. For these Reasons, the Trade of a *Soldier* is held
the most honourable of all others: Because a *Soldier* is a *Yahoo* hired
to kill in cold Blood as many of his own species, who have never
offended him, as possibly he can.

(ch. 5)

Even in so opinionated a passage as this one, there is still a centrally important sense in which Swift has the "power of remaining in uncertainty without
any irritable reaching after fact and reason." It is, one may note, a *power*, and
not a lassitude or a failure of nerve; and it is a power which is located at its
fullest only when one sees this speech as the utterance of Gulliver, facing the
Houyhnhnms, defining them dramatically for the reader by his way of facing
them, and being defined dramatically by their way of facing him. In that situation, the speech is a potent one, not as something which can (relievingly) be
attributed to Gulliver, and not as something which by its intrinsic power weighs
upon the mind of the reader, but as something in dialectic between the two.
Something at the heart of *Gulliver's Travels* is missed unless it is realized that
just such a dialectic may itself be subsumed into the "willing suspension of dis-
belief." In this present passage, to discuss the matter as if all that were in question
were the establishing of a reprehensible Gulliver or of an endorsing Swift, would
be to keep the kind of reprehensibility or of endorsement at a much more superficial level than the *Travels* as a whole establish them. One thinks, apropos a
passage of this kind, of a number of writers whose norms of engagement are
similarly complex: of Machiavelli in *The Prince*, of Dostoevsky in "The Legend
of the Grand Inquisitor," of Keats in the great Odes. In each case, a kind of
wrestle with the creatures of his own mind is the writer's best testimony to those
creatures; but then, too, they never exist apart from the wrestling. In the Swift
passage, the conclusion illuminates the whole section, and indeed the whole book,
and it is in respect of a kind of wrestling that it is done. This becomes clearer if
one considers the end of this last section, "It is a very kingly, honourable, and
frequent Practice . . . as possibly he can."

It has a number of easily noticed rhetorical and reductive elements in it.
The opening, "It is a very kingly, honourable, and frequent Practice," is one,
with its accommodation of the first couple of adjectives to the third. The con-

tinual closing of the gap between description and injunction is another example, working with skilful variety in "Allyance by Blood or Marriage, is a sufficient Cause of War between Princes," and in "and Pride and Hunger will ever be at Variance." A third example is the telescoping movement of that same sentence, by which blood or marriage are connected with pride and hunger via the inverted familial status of nations. Most strikingly though, and most importantly, there is the concluding sentence. The crucial word here is "Yahoo," not mainly because one is impelled to ask whether soldiers in real life can be described as such, nor because one is convinced that the Gulliverian soldier of this passage must inevitably be described as such, but precisely because the word is here a point of crystallization of both questions, the one in terms of the other. The truth about princes, war and soldiers, and the fidelity of a Gulliverian approximation to that truth, are questioned most taxingly and most economically in the placing of that one word.

That it can be so questioned is due to a correlation between the spirit of this passage as an isolated unity, and the context in which it is set. Within the passage, up to and including the last sentence, the spirit is one of aphorism infused by argument—a spirit which, when allowed unmitigated play, is easily felt as peculiarly authoritative. It is also a spirit which tends to be elitist, intellectually intensive, and somewhat solitary in the very act of address and communication —hence, among other things, the relevance of adducing *The Prince* and "The Legend of the Grand Inquisitor." In the Swift passage, all of this works about the last sentence, where Gulliver summarily interprets the whole of princely and soldierly practice in terms of the Yahoos, but implicitly insists that the Yahoos as known to the Houyhnhnms fall short of the peculiar malevolence of the Europeans: "hired to kill in cold Blood as many of his own species" is the relevant touch here. In this, he is at one with the Houyhnhnm his master, who several times makes a similar point. But it is noteworthy not only how unironic Gulliver is in his verdict upon the Europeans, but how totally unconjecturing he is. The Houyhnhnms are presented from time to time as being a curious mixture of the supercilious and the immaculate, and they can of course be seen as being directed by quasi-totalitarian myths and impulses. But the questions put to Gulliver are real questions; and in the exchanges between Gulliver and the Houyhnhnms, Gulliver is seen as a good deal less quizzical than his master. One is to conclude, I think, not that this is a move on Swift's part towards making the Houyhnhnms more amenable beings, or even more independent rhetorical entities in the book, but that the interplay between Houyhnhnms and Gulliver is one which makes Gulliver's verdicts questionable precisely insofar as they do not themselves include any element of questioning.

None of this need be taken as suggesting what is, indeed, manifestly false —that Swift was not vehement, gripping, and "doctrinal" *in propria persona,* or that the *Travels* are a release or relief, simply from that habit of mind. It is relevant, though, to compare the effect of the last sentence of the present paragraph with a line from one of Swift's pamphlets: "Is this an Age of the World to think Crimes improbable because they are great?" The combination of aphorism and rhetorical drive in this is quite as powerful as it is in the concluding *coup* of the passage with which I am concerned here, but it contains as well a dialectic which, in the Gulliver passage, is established only when the circumstances in their fulness are taken into account. It is as stringent and as masterful as the Gulliver passage, but it is much more scrupulous: it is the more vehement for its avoidance of violence: and the note of authority is the more telling in that one senses that the speaker himself is held under a certain scrutiny and interrogation, and feels himself to be so held. And this remains true even though the whole of the Gulliver passage obviously stems from an immediacy of concern on Swift's part: there would be something critically impertinent in saying, for instance, that only part of the story about kings and soldiers is being told here, or that compassion even for these is a humane measure which must be adopted if one is not to approximate to Gulliver's or to the Houyhnhnms' state. My point is not that Gulliver's judgement is substantially awry, if it is, but that the air, manner and circumstances of that judgement are such as to submit it to a more elaborate and more interrogatory inspection.

These, then, are some of the terms on which the "Voyage to the Houyhnhnms" as a whole is defined; and it is not surprising that they accentuate the formal problem facing Swift when it comes to concluding the *Travels*. Gulliver's odyssey has to be concluded on terms appropriate to the character of that odyssey. Insofar as the issues have become more dramatic and intense, insofar as his identity becomes more precariously sustained, he can hardly be packed off home in just the way he was at the end of each of the previous three books. Nor is he allowed to go, though he says, "I here take a final Leave of my Courteous Readers, and return to enjoy my own Speculations in my little Garden at *Redriff*." The phrases immediately following give the courteous readers pause:

> to apply those excellent Lessons of Virtue which I learned among the
> *Houyhnhnms*; to instruct *Yahoos* of my own Family as far as I shall
> find them docible Animals; to behold my Figure often in a Glass,
> and thus if possible habituate my self by Time to tolerate the Sight of
> a human Creature.
>
> (ch. 12)

The really fascinating part of this is, I think, "to behold my Figure often in a Glass, and thus if possible habituate my self by Time to tolerate the sight of a human Creature." It is one of those images which show Swift's imaginative economy to such good effect: an image like that of the gigantic skeleton in Lilliput, or that of the white staff in Brobdingnag, as tall as the mast of the *Royal Sovereign*. More notably than either of these, though, it is an image which uses physical evocation for a more than physical point. Gulliver's contemplation of himself is, he claims, "to tolerate the Sight of a human Creature." It is clear, though, that such "toleration" will not itself be a characteristically human act but a gesture from his own superhuman security. And even that cannot be described in terms of self-love, given his difficulty in facing the mirror. The image offered by Swift is very like that implicit in Auden's comment on Narcissus: "the spell in which he is trapped is not a desire for himself but the satisfaction of not desiring the nymphs." It is closely reminiscent too of an epigram of Pope's, written with Swift psychologically, at least, at hand: "There are some solitary wretches, who seem to have left the rest of mankind, only as Eve left Adam, to meet the devil in private."

It is in this context that the most acute irony of the book emerges. It is this Gulliver—tortured by the prospect of human beings, yet oddly complicit with the torture, since he takes it for a guarantee of his moral superiority—this Gulliver who reviles pride in the concluding passages of the book. For him, the "due course of things" is tolerable enough, even when it is the due course of vice. Something else baffles and infuriates him. Speaking of pride, he offers his last essay in self-definition:

> But the *Houyhnhnms*, who live under the Government of Reason, are no more proud of the good Qualities they possess, than I should be for not wanting a Leg or an Arm, which no Man in his Wits would boast of, although he must be miserable without them. I dwell the longer upon this Subject from the Desire I have to make the Society of an *English Yahoo* by any Means not insupportable; and therefore I here entreat those who have any Tincture of this absurd Vice, that they will not presume to appear in my Sight.
>
> (ch. 12)

This is the last and most brilliant of Swift's "contradictions" of man in the *Travels*: Gulliver is made at last to speak the truth, a truth to which he is the untiring claimant, and which he does not even begin to comprehend. The essential pride in question here is not an additional or even a culminating vice: it is the persuasion of self-sufficiency which gives rise to all possible vices and sustains them, providing them with rationale. Gulliver, in taking for granted his position of absolute moral command, is not only logically absurd when he reviles pride, but is the most extreme possible instance of that pride. To take oneself for *animal rationale* instead of *animal rationis capax*, and to revile the incidental absurdities of being the latter is, in Swift's view, the strongest possible evidence for one's being *rationis capax*, someone who stumbles into and out of reason.

In a way, then, the Publisher was right, and Gulliver himself was right, in making those large claims for veracity. He does tell the truth, even though it is a truth he cannot identify. And it is appropriate that the book should end just as it does: not with Gulliver settled back into business or meditation or preparing for a further voyage, but with him caught in a gesture of protest. Essentially, the *Travels* are not about the places he went to, but about the place he did not go to: the self. And they end with him stranded, simply and forever and in ignorance of the territory, *there*. He did indeed leave the rest of mankind to meet the devil in private; but he never learned that, in private, the devil's name is Gulliver.

All turns, though, on the nature of that "privacy"; and clearly Swift's alternative to it is not one of an ideal "publicity." As I have pointed out, the bespeaking and intensifying of identity on Gulliver's part is mainly by way of approximation and negation. He assembles, reassembles, dissembles; and in Swift's hands he does so less as a moral agent or patient than as a configuration of agency and patience. If it emerges so often in the *Travels* that, on Swift's view, to be man is in the end dangerously close to be playing at man, it is no surprise that the ending should have the character it has. What I called earlier the "wrestling" goes on to the end, for Swift is interested, perhaps in spite of himself, not only in illuminating the drama of the human state, but in heightening it. And given his understanding of that state, the heightening inevitably consists in an intensification at once of the Gulliverian comedy and the Gulliverian tragedy—and in a binding of the reader more closely to that situation as the book comes to its conclusion. Had Gulliver been a consistently constructed character, figure or "personality" in the work, this would not have been possible in the way that, in the event, it is. One would then have been left with some such reflection, and with some such possibility of retreat or surmounting, as there is in Montaigne's observation in his essay, "That we laugh and cry for the same thing":

> Were it not the sign of a fool to talk to one's self, there would hardly
> be a day or hour wherein I might not be heard to grumble, and
> mutter to my self and against my self; "sham'd in the fool's teeth,"
> and yet I do not think that to be my character.

As things stand with Gulliver, though, the intellectual, emotional and moral dilemmas into which he has come by the end of the book are not conceptually resolvable. Gulliver has come to be propounded as a being, a voice, a disposition of life not so much over against the reader as somehow in him. The last chapter of the "Houyhnhnms" is the masterpiece of the whole work, and one index of this is that to call it (for instance) "tragi-comedy" is to fall indefinitely short of describing either the literary mode or the intellectual preoccupation. It is the product of a mind knowing itself to be called, by its perspicacity, into a scarifying portrayal of the limits of perspicacity. All the more striking, then, that in the face of the tragic impulse the comedy does not become wan, and in the face of the comic impulse, the tragedy does not become diffident. There are not many works I know of that strike one throughout as both deliberative and dancing, but *Gulliver's Travels* is surely one of these. It may be, then, that the nearest imaginative equivalent to Swift's is not any of the works which deal benignly or ironically with Utopia, but the work of another ambiguously Irish writer, proclaiming with skill and pain but not without gaiety that

> as a result of the labours left unfinished crowned by the Acacacacademy of Essy-in-Possy of Testew and Cunard it is established beyond all doubt all other doubt than that which clings to the labours of men that as a result of the labours unfinished of Testew and Cunard it is established as hereinafter but not so fast for reasons unknown that as a result of the public works of Puncher and Wattmann it is established beyond all doubt that in view of the labours of Fartov and Belcher left unfinished for reasons unknown of Testew and Cunard left unfinished it is established what many deny that man in Possy of Testew and Cunard that man in Essy that man in short that man in brief in spite of the strides of alimentation and defecation is seen to waste and pine waste and pine.

DAVID NOKES

Swift and the Beggars

It is a very melancholy Reflection, that such a Country as ours . . .
should yet lye under the heaviest Load of Misery and Want, our
Streets crouded with Beggars, so many of our lower Sort of Trades-
men, Labourers and Artificers, not able to find Cloaths and Food for
their Families.

Whereabouts in Swift's work does this come from? From *A Modest Proposal*,
perhaps? Well, not quite, but here is the opening of that work for comparison.

It is a melancholly Object to those, who walk through this great
Town, or travel in the Country; when they see the *Streets*, the *Roads*
and *Cabbin-doors* crowded with *Beggars* of the Female Sex.

The verbal similarities are obvious, but are they more than coincidental? In fact
the first passage is taken from Swift's sermon on the *Causes of the Wretched
Condition of Ireland*. As with the other sermons, there is no precise way to date
the composition of this piece, yet the subject matter itself suggests the early 1720s,
and it is quite conceivable that Swift borrowed phrases and descriptions from a
sermon which was not intended for publication, for incorporation into *A Modest
Proposal*, which was. Indeed, it would have been remarkable had there been no
such similarities between two works addressed to the same problem, at very much
the same time. And yet, for all this, there is something disturbing about the facility
with which Swift is able to employ in his own sermons the same phrases and
arguments which, in his satires, he attributes to modest proposers and political

From *Essays in Criticism* 26, no. 3 (July 1976). © 1976 by *Essays in Criticism*.

economists. Here are two further passages for comparison, the first from the same sermon:

> as appeareth from the vast Number of ragged and naked Children in Town and Country, led about by stroling Women, trained up in Ignorance and all Manner of Vice . . . by which numberless Families have been forced either to leave the Kingdom, or stroll about, and increase the Number of our Thieves and Beggars

and this, from A Modest Proposal:

> These *Mothers* instead of being able to work for their honest Lively-hood, are forced to employ all their Time in stroling to beg Sustenance for their *helpless Infants*; who, as they grow up, either turn *Thieves* for want of Work; or leave their *dear Native Country, to fight for the Pretender in* Spain, or sell themselves to the *Barbadoes*.

Swift is literature's great ventriloquist, and we have come to recognise that understanding his works is a matter of distinguishing the master's voice from those of his puppet personae. *A Modest Proposal* is often produced as a *locus classicus* of his mature ironic style. In it he challenges us to register our own humanity by supplying those humane qualities which his rhetorical and logical formulae deliberately leave out of account. Yet in accepting this challenge we must beware of allowing our liberal principles to prejudice our understanding of what Swift must have meant, supplying lacunae where none was left, and laying virtues to Swift's charge of which he was not guilty. The sermons demonstrate many of Swift's positive beliefs, and they are not of a kind to warm the hearts of humanitarians. It is true that the sermons do not give us the whole man; they are specifically tailored for their small parish audience, and when Swift heard that his successor at Kilroot, having found the sermons, proposed to make further use of them, he tried to dissuade him with these disclaimers:

> They were what I was firmly resolved to burn. . . . They will be a perfect lampoon upon me, whenever you look upon them, and re-member they are mine.

Although we may not necessarily see them as lampoons on the rest of Swift's work, the sermons certainly reveal Swift in an uncharacteristically sober guise. As Louis Landa writes:

> Swift had a modest and conservative conception of what preaching should accomplish—"to tell the people what is their duty, and to convince them that it is so," and to do this without oratory or dis-plays of learning, by "sober Sense and plain Reason." What then

was better suited to his purpose than the unembellished Christian truths which had stood the test of time, a conservative adherence to simple and indisputable orthodoxy as he conceived it? Thus we need not be surprised to find that he often relies upon the truisms and commonplaces of Christian thought, such as came from countless clergymen of his own and preceding generations.

This principle of adhering to orthodox themes and expressions in his sermons was seconded by a more cynical strain of pragmatism, however, since Swift had already learnt the cost of eccentricity. Smarting from the reputation for blasphemy that he had gained from the publication of *A Tale of a Tub*, he remarks of the clergy:

> to whose Preferment nothing is so fatal as the Character of Wit, Politeness in Reading, or Manners, or that Kind of Behaviour which we contract by having too much conversed with Persons of high Station and Eminency; these Qualifications being reckoned by the *Vulgar of all Ranks* to be Marks of *Levity*, which is the last Crime the world will pardon in a *Clergy-Man*.

It is notoriously difficult to delineate the positive values behind Swift's satires, but can we confidently consign his sermons to the antiquarian corner as clerical hackwork, the rote-like deployment of familiar texts and glosses?

Swift's sermons are homilies on social rather than spiritual topics. They seek to encourage dutiful behaviour and orthodox opinions by eschewing the theological problems and recommending instead of a simple, deferential and conservative code of conduct to his parishioners. The sermon on the *Causes of the Wretched Condition of Ireland* lists four main causes of present distress; vanity, luxury, idleness and the avarice of landlords. The dominant strain that runs through the sermon is a puritan insistence upon the virtue of self-reliance. Charges are levelled against those, mainly women, who "in the midst of Poverty, are suffered to run into all Kinds of Expence and Extravagance" and against those so given over to idleness that "they often chuse to beg or steal, rather than support themselves with their own labor." It is an axiom of Swift's social philosophy that social ills have their origins in moral failings, and that social stability depends on hard work and self-sufficiency—moral virtues in their own right. As a partial solution he proposes the establishment of a network of charity schools in which children may be taught "to think and act according to the Rules of Reason, by which a spirit of Industry and Thrift and Honesty would be introduced among them." He goes on:

> In all industrious Nations, Children are looked on as a Help to their Parents, with us, for want of being early trained to work, they are an

> intolerable Burthen at Home, and a grievous Charge upon the Public,
> as appeareth from the vast Number of ragged and naked Children.

"People are the riches of a Nation"—so ran the pious commonplace; but in real life this was not always so—at least not all people. Gregory King's census figures for England in 1688 drew a deliberate and invidious line between those families which increased the wealth of the nation, according to contemporary notions, and those which impoverished it. The number below the line was disconcertingly high—849,000 families decreasing the wealth of the nation, and only 511,586 families above the line striving to increase that wealth. In fact the great *per capita* income of those above the line left the nation with a healthy surplus of £1,825,100 —but the implication of that sharp line drawn between getters and spenders was a sombre one. And this was England. Very few of the substantial families living in Ireland could make up the deficit created by hundreds of thousands of beggars throughout the country. Both Swift in his sermon, and the Modest Proposer in his, address themselves to the problem of raising the children of the Irish poor over that line, so that they might cease to be a national burden, and become a national asset.

> I think it is agreed by all Parties, that this prodigious Number of
> Children in Arms, or on the Backs, or at the Heels of their Mothers,
> and frequently of their Fathers, is in the present deplorable State of
> the Kingdom, a very great additional Grievance; and therefore, who-
> ever could find out a fair, cheap, and easy Method of making these
> Children sound and useful Members of the Commonwealth, would
> deserve so well of the Publick, as to have his Statue set up for a
> Preserver of the Nation.

Swift hopes that a sound moral education will do the trick; the Modest Proposer's ideas are considerably more radical; yet their economic premisses are the same. Neither invokes compassion or conscience as relevant considerations in analysing the situation of the poor. There are strict limits to the application of Christian charity in social matters, and Swift goes out of his way to justify the division of the world into rich and poor.

> But, before I proceed farther, let me humbly presume to vindicate the
> Justice and Mercy of God and his Dealings with Mankind. Upon
> this Particular He hath not dealt so hardly with his Creatures as some
> would imagine, when they see so many miserable Objects ready to
> perish for Want: For it would infallibly be found, upon strict Enquiry,
> that there is hardly one in twenty of those miserable Objects who do
> not owe their present Poverty to their own Faults, to their present

> Sloth and Negligence; to their indiscreet Marriage without the least
> Prospect of supporting a Family, to their foolish Expensiveness, to
> their Drunkenness, and other Vices, by which they have squandered
> their Gettings, and contracted Diseases in their old Age.

And, in his sermon *On the Poor Man's Contentment*, which is devoted specifically to this topic, Swift strains the quality of his charity even further.

> But here I would not be misunderstood; perhaps, there is not a Word
> more abused than that of the Poor, or wherein the World is more
> generally mistaken. Among the Number of those who beg in our
> Streets, or are half starved at Home, or languish in Prison for Debt,
> there is hardly one in a hundred who doth not owe his Misfortunes
> to his own Laziness or drunkenness, or worse Vices.
>
> To these he owes those very Diseases which often disable him from
> getting his Bread. Such Wretches are deservedly unhappy; they can
> only blame themselves; and when we are commanded to have Pity
> on the Poor, these are not understood to be of their Number.

There is something unpleasantly pharisaical about the smug formula "deservedly
unhappy," which Swift applies to ninety-nine in every hundred of the beggars he
meets. It is a distasteful inversion of the parable of the lost sheep when Swift's
concern is not for the one in a hundred who has fallen, but exclusively for the
one in a hundred who is pure.

> For by the Poor I only intend the honest, industrious Artificer, the
> meaner Sort of Tradesmen, and the labouring Man, who getteth his
> Bread by the Sweat of his Brow.

It is by these clichés—the sweating brow rather than the idle drunkard—that
Swift regulates his conscience and his charity. He is determined to identify finan-
cial distress with moral culpability. His language is charged with moral oppro-
brium, and he sees poverty as the outward and visible sign of sinfulness. Hence
compassion is ruled out of court as an accessory to the original vice that has
brought the individual to penury. And without the intercession of compassion,
Swift is working with the same economic logic that presents itself to his Modest
Proposer.

The prodigal son is another of the compassionate parables that finds no
place in Swift's philosophy.

> And, to speak freely, is it any Way reasonable or just, that those who
> have denied themselves many lawful Satisfactions and Conveniences
> of Life, from a Principle of Conscience, as well as Prudence, that they

> might not be a Burthen to the Public, should be charged with sup-
> porting Others, who have brought themselves to less than a Morsel
> of Bread by their Idleness, Extravagance, and Vice?

Even the old and infirm have no real claim upon his charity.

> For the Artificer or other Tradesman, who pleadeth he is grown too
> old to work or look after Business, and therefore expecteth Assistance
> as a decayed Housekeeper; may we not ask him, why did he not take
> Care in his Youth and Strength of Days, to make some provision
> against old Age, when he saw so many Examples before him of People
> undone by their Idleness and vicious Extravagance?

This is a case where one might have wished Swift had used some of the modest
computation he puts to such good effect in his satires to determine how much an
"honest industrious Artificer" might have been expected to put by for his old age
in the contemporary economic conditions. But in this sermon he is clearly not
concerned with such practical details. It is all put down to vice and vanity—no
other explanation will do. Only when he has established this impregnable position of moral absolutism does Swift concede that there are weaker brethren whose
distress is not wholly of their own making and who do not entirely deserve their
misery. It is these "whom it is chiefly incumbent upon us to support." There is a
complete lack of spontaneity about that response. Relief is admitted as a duty
since "we are commanded to have pity on the poor," but it is to be administered
wholly without compassion or enthusiasm. There is no joy in fulfilling the commandment to succour the poor, since Swift's reactions are coloured by his belief
that at root, fecklessness and vanity are the causes of hunger. His charity is therefore suspicious and grudging. Economic ills, like all other hardships, are part of
the lot which fallen man must endure.

To err on the side of generosity is to err on the side of vice, and all Swift's
energies are directed to ensuring that charity is only made available to that one in
a hundred of the truly deserving poor.

> To turn our Charity into its proper Channel, we ought to consider
> who and where those Objects are, whom it is chiefly incumbent upon
> us to support.

The scheme which he envisages for regulating charity is thoroughly penal in style,
since his main objectives are to enforce the humility of those receiving alms, and
to free the city of Dublin of the burden and incumbrance of interlopers and stroll-
ing beggars who were properly the concern of the outlying parishes.

> For if every Parish could take a List of those begging Poor which
> properly belong to it, and compel each of them to wear a Badge,

marked and numbered, so as to be seen and known by all they meet, and confine them to beg within the Limits of their own Parish, severally punishing them when they offend, and driving out all Interlopers from other Parishes, we could then make a Computation of their Numbers, and the Strolers from the Country being driven away, the Remainder would not be too many for the Charity of those who pass by, to maintain.

The parable of the "good Samaritan" is thus the third to find no place in Swift's treatment of the poor. The neighbour whom he feels enjoined to love must reside within the pale of Dublin city.

Even with these limits Swift found it impossible to believe he was actually required to *love* his neighbour. This was a commandment which caused him real heart-searching, conflicting as it did so directly with the pose of misanthropy which he adopted as an externalisation of those very intense feelings of hostility which he had for many facets of contemporary society. In his sermon, *On Doing Good*, Swift faces up to this question with some bold opening assertions:

> We are . . . commanded to love our Neighbours as ourselves, but not as well as ourselves. The love we have for ourselves is to be the pattern of that love we ought to have towards our neighbour: But as the copy doth not equal the original, so my neighbour cannot think it hard, if I prefer myself, who am the original, before him, who is only the copy.

This is a highly revealing piece of scriptural exegesis, and as fine an example of apologetic reasoning as one could hope to find in the works of any of the neo-Aristotelian church fathers. In another context—in *A Tale of a Tub* for instance—one would applaud such a passage as a neat ironic parody of clerical casuistry. For what we have here is the conversion of a commandment to altruistic behaviour, into a confirmation of egocentricity. The centrifugal force of the commandment has been made centripetal. This is a valuable glimpse of Swift's conscience at work, trying to reconcile his dogmatic faith with his psychology which did not, could not, cease to put *self* first. His adherence to the cynical philosophy of La Rochefoucauld was more than a pose, yet he would not admit that his own deepest instincts—instincts which he believed were common to all men—were contrary to a central article of the Christian faith. So he offers this ingenious reinterpretation of the commandment to de-sublime its demands. The word as in "Love they neighbour as thyself" is made to do quite as much work as the word "end" in his virtuoso punning performance on the injunction to "regard thy end" in the "Digression in praise of Digressions" from a *Tale of a Tub*. But here the full weight of the defensive obsession behind the ingenuity is felt in a

way we only dimly suspect at the back of the rhetorical pyrotechnics of the earlier
work.

This interpretation agrees with the tendency of the sermons as a whole
which is to dismiss or deride theological disputes while enjoining practical conformity within the Anglican church, and stressing the heavenly rewards for such
conformity. Swift wishes to make it easier for both himself and his parishioners
to believe that which it is necessary for them to believe for their own salvation.
"Human nature is so constituted, that we can never pursue any thing heartily but
upon hopes of a reward," he writes in his sermon *On the Excellency of Christianity*, where consequently his endeavour is to promote the Anglican church as a
"best buy." He is particularly scathing about the more sophisticated philosophers
who seek to identify the moral recompense of virtue itself.

> some of the philosophers . . . pretended to refine so far, as to call virtue
> its own reward, and worthy to be followed only for itself: Whereas,
> if there be anything in this more than the sound of the words, it is at
> least too abstracted to become an universal influencing principle in
> the world, and therefore could not be of general use.

So crude does this argument of "general use" appear to us in a spiritual context
that we look for a hint of irony in those quasi-chemical terms, "abstracted" and
"refined"—terms which Swift puts to such good effect in several of his satires.
But there is none of that playfulness here. In the interests of general use and
orthodoxy Swift is prepared to deride Thales, Solon, Aristotle, Plato, Zeno and
Epicurus as benighted heretics caught up with the casuistry of virtue being its
own reward when only membership of the Anglican church can ensure eternal
happiness.

It is not surprising, then, that *A Modest Proposal* and the sermon on the
Causes of the Wretched Condition of Ireland should display not only coincidental similarities of phraseology but basic similarities in their underlying attitudes
and assumptions. As Donoghue observes, there is a tendency in considering the
works of Swift to underestimate the element of non-irony, and read all the plus
signs as minuses. *A Modest Proposal* is such a monstrous exhibition of inhumanity that, in compensation, we tend to decode it by converting the force of its
energy into an equally impressive monument of compassion. However, it is perfectly possible, indeed probable, that the work should still retain a number of
those minor inhumanities which we have now swept away in our dislike of means
tests and the moral attitudes they imply. Compare this passage:

> Some Persons of a desponding Spirit are in great Concern about that
> vast Number of poor People, who are Aged, Diseased, or Maimed;
> and I have been desired to employ my Thoughts what Course may

be taken, to ease the Nation of so grievous an Incumbrance. But I am
not in the least Pain upon the Matter; because it is very well known,
that they are every Day *dying*, and rotting, by *Cold* and *Famine* and
Filth, and *Vermin*, as fast as can be reasonably expected. And as to
the younger Labourers, they are now in almost as hopeful a Condition; They cannot get Work, and consequently pine away for Want
of Nourishment, to a Degree, that if at any time they are accidently
hired to common Labour, they have not Strength to perform it; and
thus the Country, and themselves, are in a fair Way of being soon
delivered from the Evils to come

with this, from *Causes of the Wretched Condition of Ireland*:

Yet, it is certain, that there are very many who publickly declare they
will never wear those Badges, and many others who either hide or
throw them away: But the Remedy for this is very short, easy and
just, by tying them like Vagabonds and sturdy Beggars, and forcibly
driving them out of Town. Therefore, as soon as this Expedient of
wearing Badges shall be put in Practice, I do earnestly exhort all
those who hear me, never to give their Alms to any publick Beggar
who doth not fully comply with this Order; by which our Number
of Poor will be so reduced, that it will no longer crouded with so
many Thieves and Pick-pockets, in Beggars Habits, nor our Streets
so dangerous to those who are forced to walk in the Night.

In both passages we find the same determined simplification of a problem; a
truculent insistence upon cutting through the Gordian knot that more tender-
conscienced treatment will only complicate. The deliberate brutality of the modest
proposer's "I am not in the least Pain upon this Matter" is paralleled by Swift's
own assertion, "the Remedy for this is very short, easy and just." They are the
kind of assertions that demand an end of further argument. A second similarity
is in the coaxing tone that accompanies these assertions, which seeks to assure us
that all is for the best; that starving labourers are in a "hopeful condition" and
that alms ought never to be given to beggars not wearing the parish badge.

The modest proposer's language suggests the activities of conscience: "I
have been desired to employ my thoughts what Course may be taken to ease the
Nation of so grievous an Incumbrance." But it is the Nation that must be eased,
not the suffering. Like most political theorists, the proposer assumes a distinction
between the nation and those who comprise it. The word "ease" is a typical
Swiftian usage. Had the proposer said "rid the Nation" he would have seemed so
much less modest. "Ease" naturally suggests the easing of pains and, by associa-
tion, we feel he must be proposing to ease the burden of the poor. Yet even that

paraphrase indicates the nature of the ambiguity Swift exploits, since it may mean either "the burden suffered by the poor" or "the burden imposed upon the nation by the poor." The proposer seems modest by sounding as though he means the first, while applying his remedies to the second. The fact that he is "not in the least Pain upon the Matter" emphasises his remoteness from the real pains of those he discusses: "it is very well known that they are every day dying and rotting by cold and famine, and filth and vermin; as fast as can be reasonably expected."

The economic logic is flawless; reverse the assumption that life is of pre-eminent importance and cold and famine become handy political instruments for ending unemployment "as fast as can be reasonably expected." The younger labourers are "now in almost as hopeful a Condition"—hopeful to the nation that is—since they are caught in what contemporary jargon would call a recessionary spiral:

> They cannot get work, and consequently pine away for want of Nourishment, to a degree that if at any time they are accidentally hired to common labour, they have not strength to perform it, and thus the country and themselves are happily delivered from the evils to come.

"Reasonably expect," "hopeful a condition," "happily delivered"—these confidential and restrained qualifications maintain the modest tone of a man with everyone's good at heart, while his argument unfolds the most calculated callousness. For the proposer is a complex character. Swift does not make him completely obtuse to the hideous implications of what he suggests. There is a nervous cough in his voice—"I shall now therefore humbly propose my own Thought, which I hope will not be liable to the least Objection"—which entreats us into a conspiracy of silence. It's a mealymouthed nervousness that wishes to be absolved from any unmentioned or unmentionable offensiveness in what is proposed, and we sense a guilty consciousness in his institutional declarations of humanity that excuse him from any real responsibility or concern. Later, when introducing refinements to his basic scheme regarding ways of serving children at table, he includes one "by a very worthy Person and true Lover of his Country" for supplying the shortage of venison with specially reared children of between twelve and fourteen years, but demurs in his greasy fashion, for "it is not improbable that some scrupulous People might be apt to censure such a practice (although very unjustly) as a little bordering on cruelty; which I confess, hath always been with me the strongest Objection against my Project, how well soever intended." Yet this objection is only raised after three material considerations have already caused him to reject the idea; the cost of maintaining children till twelve; the toughness of their flesh, "like that of our schoolboys"; and the waste of a capital asset in slaughtering females just when they would be ready to breed themselves.

It's this obsequious strain of guilt-consciousness that gives the proposer's ideas their real obscenity. He is not simply an absentminded theorist so used to dealing with statistics that he *cannot* think of people as people. Such a figure, while yielding a sense of savage farce, would be innocent of *conscious* evil. But there's a shiftiness, a loathsome cast of political opportunism behind these proposals that takes the brunt of Swift's attack: "I fortunately fell upon this Proposal; which as it is wholly new so it hath something solid and real, of no Expense, and little Trouble, full in our own Power, and whereby we can incur no Danger of Disobliging England."

The modest proposer is in the invidious position of the Jewish police in the Warsaw ghetto, mediating between the miseries of his own people, and the intransigence of an imperial power. He is not the first to apply the strict laws of economic necessity to Ireland; he merely reacts with Pavlovian tenacity to the logic imposed by the English authorities. Yet M. B. Drapier too occupied the ambiguous positions of patriot and mediator.

> I do earnestly exhort all those who hear me, never to give their Alms to any publick Beggar who doth not fully comply with this Order by which our Number of Poor will be so reduced, that it will be no longer crouded with so many Thieves and Pickpockets in Beggars Habits.

Which master is being served here? Just as the modest proposer depersonalises the poor into "dams" and "breeders," so in the sermon Swift thus devalues their distress, describing it as a "beggar's habit" which disguises thieves and pickpockets. What is the logic of this proposal "by which our Number of Poor will be so reduced . . . ?" "Reduced" can only mean either that they will have gone elsewhere—which is no solution at all, but simply an expedient to make their sufferings no longer our problem—or that a solution is envisaged which is unstated—as it must be. Swift too begs us into a conspiracy of high-minded silence. By regulating charity in this manner the numbers of the poor will be reduced "as fast as can be reasonably expected" by the same agencies of cold, famine, filth and vermin that the modest proposer relies upon. For the crucial similarity between Swift's tone and that of the proposer is that both see the problem from the viewpoint of the hard-pressed alms-giver called upon to support an idle population. There is never any consideration of the situation from the view of the beggars themselves. Their poverty disenfranchises them—they are not part of the political nation, and must submit to what is done too them and for them. It is the burden which the poor impose upon the nation and upon him as a taxpayer, not the burden which the poor themselves suffer, which Swift, like the proposer, feels the need to remedy. This similarity leads to those unintended ironies in his use of such terms as burden, incumbrance, ease and reduce.

None of his Irish tracts reveals any real sense of identification between Swift and those he claimed to represent. On the contrary he often expresses contempt for the shortsighted expedients and indolence of a population unable to recognise its own interests. What he did gain from his involvement in Irish politics was a platform from which to confront his old enemies of the Whig establishment in England. In his letters of this period one notes a return of the conspiratorial excitement that characterised his correspondence during the hectic days of Harley's administration. He is to become a name once more; "As soon as it is heard that I have been with folks in power, they get twenty stories about the town of what has passed." In the constitutional debate over the status of Ireland as a "dependent" kingdom Swift has his revenge on the "great folks" in England in the kind of legalistic argument that always stimulated his finest rhetoric. It would be wrong, of course, to ignore the many positive and practical remedies which Swift proposed to the economic problems of Ireland, remedies concerned with the protection and encouragement of Irish manufacturing, with reducing the expropriation of Irish revenues and resources to England. Yet on the specific problem of beggars in the streets, we should not exaggerate his humanitarian concern.

Kathleen Williams concludes from *A Modest Proposal*, that "moral and humane behaviour may, for Swift, contribute to the true well-being of a state." Yet the real intensity of the pamphlet derives from Swift's desire to confront the English authorities with their own insensitivity by bringing their abstractions to life at the moment of being "dressed hot from the knife." There is no one better than he at highlighting the squirming evasions that lurk within political euphemisms, at exposing the callous indifference of English authorities and the cynical opportunism of rack-renting absentee landlords. Yet, when required to declare his own position, as in the sermons, we find a strain of economic thinking not at all dissimilar from that practised by the English authorities themselves; a form of self-help mercantilism which identifies the ability to survive economically as a sign or moral probity. Thus, while he advocated certain sound and sensible reforms for the problems of Ireland, Swift himself seized upon the economic miseries of Ireland in an opportunist fashion, as an issue which would bring him back to political prominence.

As a final proof of his probity the modest proposer makes this declaration of disinterestedness: "I have no Children by which I can propose to get a single Penny; the youngest being nine years old, and my wife past child-bearing." Swift was always distrustful of those who claimed to act from disinterested motives, and proclaimed La Rochefoucauld "my Favorite because I found my whole character in him." There is a tendency to view such declarations as this as ironic exaggeration; yet beyond the pose of misanthropy there is an even more characteristic Swiftian device here—that of truth-telling in such a provocative manner that one is certain to be disbelieved. Swift held seriously to the belief that self-interest was the basic human motive, and his concern as a clergyman was to expound a code of behaviour and belief that recognised the fact, and a moral system of sticks and carrots to enforce it. So it is hardly surprising if self-interest entered into his political writings. A desire to vex the Whig establishment was not at odds with a wish to reduce the exploitation of Irish industries and estates. It is a good example of self-love and social proving the same. Swift's own explanation of his own misanthropy is well known:

> I have ever hated all Nations professions and Communityes and all my love is towards individualls, for instance I hate the tribe of lawyers, but I love Councellor such a one . . . but principally I hate and detest that animal called man, although I hartily love John, Peter, Thomas and so forth.

It is quite consistent for him to extend this orthodox conservative distrust of abstractions of all kinds to a hatred of the tribe of beggars, and to single out for his charity the one in a hundred with a human face, while dismissing the rest as mere statistics.

SUSAN GUBAR

The Female Monster
in Augustan Satire

"A woman in the shape of a monster," Adrienne Rich observes in *Planetarium*, "a monster in the shape of a woman / the skies are full of them." And the skies must have seemed just as full of female monsters to writers like Djuna Barnes, Carson McCullers, Isak Dinesen, Robin Morgan, and May Sarton. They were also sensitive to their cultural inheritance, and female monsters have long inhabited the male imagination, a monitory image of female creativity and a testimony to the misogyny of our literary past. At no time were these female grotesques more prevalent than during the eighteenth century. Emblems of filthy materiality, committed only to their private ends, the decaying prostitutes portrayed by Jonathan Swift in his excremental poetry are quite literally monsters whose arts are both debased and debasing. In the representation of male dread of women and, more specifically, of male anxiety over female control and artistry, Swift's contaminating bitch goddesses evoke a long line of female monsters of biblical and classical origin, not to mention those who abound in the antiromantic satire of the other Scriblerians.

Rather than confront these characters, male critics like Norman O. Brown and Donald Greene attempt to provide Swift with justifications in an apparent effort to salvage the poet's reputation from charges of sexual neuroses and anal anxiety. Brown's famous chapter on "The Excremental Vision" in *Life against Death* argues that the poet was in fact a proto-Freud, describing the process of sublimation that constitutes culture. For Greene, however, the scatological poems are not Freudian but Christian: they affirm the *un*importance of the fact that

From *Signs: Journal of Women in Culture and Society* 3, no. 2 (Winter 1977). © 1977 by The University of Chicago.

"Caelia shits!" Could Swift himself have better set up a satire on criticism than by creating two critics named Brown and Greene to explicate poems about female feces and male vanity? But Swift would not have added a third, yet more quarrelsome voice—a woman's voice—to this debate, because women do not have voices in his poetic world. What they do have is messy rooms filled with filthy combs, putrid potions, and sweaty castoffs—all observed by Strephon in *The Lady's Dressing Room* (1730). They have, especially after drinking twelve consecutive cups of tea, the need to relieve themselves that overcomes the heroine of *Strephon and Chloe* (1731) on her wedding night. And yes, to the consternation of the eponymous Cassinus and Peter (1731), they excrete. Brown and Greene focus on these three poems as a closed set, especially on the comments made in the poet's own voice. Brown associates this voice with the horror experienced by the male characters, their enlightened consciousness of anality or truth. Swift, it would appear, was outraged that civilized behavior is only a veneer concealing the grossest physicality. Greene, on the other hand, dissociating the characters from the poet, claims that Swift is satirizing male egoism and female pretension that together produce an absurdly inadequate reaction in men and women against the human condition.

But the experience of reading the three poems contradicts both of these paradigms. Swift does not dismiss Western civilization as mere sublimation, nor does he bless the body as part of God's creation. Instead, in these and other poems, Swift describes his own inability to accept the ambiguities and contradictions of the human condition, portraying his failure in the figure of the repulsive female. Like disgusted Gulliver, who returns to England only to prefer the stable to the parlor and his horses to his wife, the satirist projects his horror of time, his dread of physicality, onto another stinking creature—the degenerate woman.

These poems and the satires of the other Scriblerians can also be viewed as a tacit admission that the woman's way, the way of death, is a seductive/destructive alternative to the difficult task of mediating among biological, spiritual, and social needs. Swift's poetry thus provides a useful framework for understanding the meaning and function of the female monster in male-created literature.

Swift's *Cassinus and Peter* is a poem about two friends, undergraduates, who meet to talk about love and literature. Cassinus bemoans a crime committed by Caelia that had led him to a very literary and inflated sense of inconsolable woe. Although we learn with Peter that Caelia has not died, turned prostitute, or succumbed to the pox, it is only in the last line of the poem that we discover the "Crime that shocks all human Kind" (63): "Caelia shits!" If female reality is pretty grim, male illusions and standards are ridiculous. In the initial description, Cassinus wears a greasy stocking on his head, a ragged shirt, and torn breeches which fail to hide legs "well embrown'd with Dirt and Hair" (18). His passion

for Caelia's purity, then, in ridiculous in light of his own filthiness which, as
Greene points out, serves to deflate his rhapsodic language; we are meant to see
how double his standards are. Cassinus's idealization of his mistress is based on
ignorance not only of her anatomy but of his own sloth. Furthermore, this idealization masks his fear of the other sex: when he imagines his own death, with
appropriate elegies and sonnets, he pictures an encounter in the underworld with
one of the oldest female monsters: "I come, I come,—*Medusa*, see, / Her Serpents
hiss direct at me" (85–86). Swift is undoubtedly satirizing male romanticism
through Cassinus, but in the process he seizes the opportunity to unmask the
Medusa behind the Muse invoked at the start of the poem. Indeed there is ultimately a crucial difference between the attacks on Cassinus and on Caelia. Ludicrous as Cassinus's views of women are, they are harmless, whimsically appropriate in a college soph, and they can presumably be corrected. But how can Caelia
ever learn to escape her faults when they are equated with her bodily functions—
especially when these are all that define her in Swift's world? Although he recognizes Caelia's right to excrete, Swift is also horrified by it. And although he ridicules Cassinus's literary romanticism, he apprehends the motives and impulses
behind it—namely, Caelia's fall into immanence, her inescapable physicality.

The deflation of romantic stereotypes and sentimental literary conventions
in *Cassinus and Peter* recurs not only in *Gulliver's Travels* (1726) but in the
work of other Augustan satirists as well. The purpose of "The Double Mistress"
episode in the *Memoirs of Martinus Scriblerus* (1741) is ostensibly just such a
deflation of female paragons—for example, the hackneyed antagonism between
a blue-eyed, golden-haired, rose-like beauty and a black-eyed, raven-haired, lily-
like heroine. Arbuthnot and Pope parody the bombastic language and the ingenious abductions that characterize second-rate literature. But as in Swift's poetry, it
is essentially the heroine's physique that serves to mock such conventions: the
blond and brunette are physically linked (Siamese) twins, members of a freak
show. Thus, when they try to escape not from their father but from their owner,
they are stuck midway in a window, one on each side, hung immodestly with
coats up to the navel. Like Swift, Arbuthnot and Pope ridicule romantic stereotypes and conventions by creating a fiction that projects male fascination and
dread of women. Their representation of Lindamira-Indamora is a symbol for
the unnatural duplicity of women that defines them as twinned freaks. Moreover,
the sexual anatomy of his awful bride creates problems for Martin, the hero. He
faces possible charges of rape, incest, and bigamy fundamentally because sexual
consummation with a woman is regarded fearfully by men as violent and un-
lawful, self-annihilating, or unnatural. The judge's first solution, that the two
husbands are "joint Proprietors of one common Tenement," evokes the dreaded
threat of homosexuality, even as it employs a traditional spatial metaphor of

female engulfment. If the confusing and contradictory marriage laws cited by both lawyers point up the inanity of jurisprudence as an institution, they also illuminate the age-old dilemma of husbands anxious for complete ownership of their wives. Indeed, since both twins are married, are not the husbands cuckolds from the start?

Exploring the ludicrous incongruities of sexuality and sentimentality, Arbuthnot and Pope use the female freak to explode the paradisal view of marriage perpetrated in romance. Whereas the sexual consent of the beautiful goddess-paragon means regeneration for the hero in romance, a satirist like Fielding in *The Tragedies of Tragedies; or, the Life and Death of Tom Thumb the Great* (1730) and *Jonathan Wild* (1743) portrays Amazon queens whose lascivious desires can never be sated by the pathetically puny heroes. These victims of lickerish females recall the child getter Filch in *The Beggar's Opera* (1728), who wastes away in Lockit's prison "like a shotten herring" (3.3). Macheath's forced acceptance of monogamy serves as the parodic happy ending of Gay's musical comedy; Macheath's alternative would be death by hanging. When Swift turns to the mock epithalamium, however, as in *Strephon and Chloe*, he shows women condemned not only by their raging appetitive drives but by their inability to control or even hide the necessities of nature successfully.

In *Strephon and Chloe*, Swift's satiric hymn to marriage, the heroine, parading as a faultless goddess, convinces her future husband that she is too divine ever to sweat or smell. But after the marriage ceremony, Chloe forgets that the wife should "keep her Spouse deluded still, / And make him fancy what she will" (143–44). Swift seems to attack Chloe for deceitful modesty before marriage and for not maintaining that same modesty after. Like all of us, Chloe must "either void or burst" (166). But "Love such Nicety requires, / One *Blast* will put out all his Fires" (135–36). Chloe is damned if she does and destroyed if she does not. When she finally discharges her "fuming rill" (175), she inspires Strephon to follow suit immediately, and all constraints soon vanish; marital intimacy degenerates very easily, it seems, into vulgar indecency. That Strephon during courtship should have witnessed Chloe's efforts and even "lickt her Leavings" (241) in order to be disabused of romantic ideas is clearly the poet's advice, not the voice of a persona later undercut by a more humanistic counselor, as Greene claims. The poet's concluding sermon on decency is informed by the same horror of female physicality that motivates the rest of the poem. When Swift warns his readers that an edifice built on sand with hay and stubble cannot last for life, he is equating female youth and beauty with crumbling, inadequate materials, "a Basis insecure" (300) that cannot sustain any structure or form. The female is compared to the foolish man who did not follow the sayings of Christ and built a house upon sand, so that it fell when the floods came (Matt. 7:27). Perhaps

Swift is working with the same biblical source that Spenser uses in his description of Lucifera's House of Pride, which is constructed of a thin layer of gold foil on a foundation of weak sand (*The Faerie Queene* [1609], 1.4.45). Because its ruinous hind parts are hard to perceive, the mansion represents the hypocrisy of both Lucifera and Duessa, who have crafted attractive fronts to cover "neather partes misshapen, monstrous" that are common to witches (1.2.41).

The secret, shameful ugliness of both Chloe and Duessa is in fact closely associated with their hidden genitals. Both descend from the daughters of Zion: when God uncovers "their secret parts" by taking away their headbands, pendants, perfumes, veils, and cloaks, "instead of sweet fragrance there shall be rottenness, and instead of a girdle, a rope; and instead of well set hair, baldness" (Isa. 3:16–24). Many readers have noted that in his dressing-room poems Swift evokes classical poets like Juvenal and Ovid, who looked behind the female facade to warn off potential male admirers. But by alluding to specifically Christian images, by referring to his readers—now explicitly men who might take wives—as "rash mortals" (301), Swift emphasizes the impious nature of female pride and deception, a theme Pope had already mined in *The Rape of the Lock* (1714). The Christian framework of Swift's concluding lines might even remind his male readers that, after all, the cause of sin and suffering can be attributed originally to female rhetorical arts, arts of pride and deception.

In the last paragraph of *Strephon and Chloe*, Swift provides a solution to the revolting revelations of marital intimacy—the prudent male must build his marriage on a sound foundation:

> On Sense and Wit your Passion found,
> By Decency cemented round;
> Let Prudence with Good Nature strive,
> To Keep Esteem and Love alive.
> Then come old Age whene'er it will,
> Your Friendship shall continue still:
> And thus a mutual gentle Fire,
> Shall never but with Life expire.
>
> (307–14)

Clearly the speaker believes in the benefits of propriety and decency, but how adequate is his solution to the problems faced by his characters earlier in the poem? Strephon and Chloe experience the horrible revelations of the wedding night precisely because decency and prudence can*not* always be maintained in the marital bed. In fact it is not a sexual relationship, not even a mature marriage that is redeemed at the conclusion of *Strephon and Chloe* but, rather, friendship between the sexes, the only kind of relationship Swift could himself tolerate with women. In this respect, *Strephon and Chloe* resembles Swift's poetry in praise of women which, as Ehrenpreis has noted, ignores physical attributes to extol, instead, moral and intellectual qualities that his society classified as masculine. For example, Swift repeatedly expresses his respect for Stella's "true Contempt for Things below" (*Stella's Birthday*, 1726/7, 69). And in *Cadenus and Vanessa* (1713), as Ehrenpreis explains, all the women are "vain, scandal-mongering, and vicious" except Vanessa, who is "defined as a miracle and not a normal woman." Even when Swift is presumably arguing in favor "Of the Education of Ladies," he focuses on the miseducation that has produced "fools, coquettes, gamesters, saunterers, endless talkers of nonsense, splenetic idlers, intriguers given to scandal and censure. . . ." The conclusion of *Strephon and Chloe* is, then, as ambiguous as many of Swift's supposedly positive works on women. Just as important a qualifier of his traditional invocation of prudence and good nature, however, is the conclusion's startling lack of realism. Nothing has been ascribed to either Strephon or Chloe that could lead us to suppose them capable of sense and wit. As is quite often the case, the satiric fiction does not quite fit the explicitly stated moral.

Like Swift, Pope praises the virtuous woman as a manly woman who has managed to transcend her sex. Pope's *Epistle to a Lady* (1735) begins in a conventional, conversational manner: "Nothing so true as what you once let fall, / 'Most Women have no Characters at all.' / Matter too soft a lasting mark to bear, / And best distinguish'd by black, brown, or fair" (1–4). Women are shown to "let fall" all kinds of things in the poem, from their clothing and china to their propriety and religion; each portrait presents a fallen woman. Composed of "Matter too soft," women are inconstant and uncommitted—"Fair to no purpose, artful to no end, / Young without Lovers, old without a Friend" (245); they epitomize folly, vanity, hypocrisy, vacancy, and sensuality. By the time Pope get to Martha Blount, his model of female excellence, he can only praise her as "a softer Man" (272). But even Martha, an "exception to all general rules" cannot escape the lack of character that paradoxically characterizes her sex. She too is destined to remain a "Contradiction" (270), an uneasy blend of antagonistic elements.

If Swift's females are also composed of "matter too soft," their physical matter is emphatically anal, and their arts are always inadequate. Instead of transmitting gross facticity, these arts can only hide it—and never successfully. In *The Lady's Dressing Room*, Caelia's stinking chamber pot is the quintessence of the room and the woman; it is reminiscent of the Whore of Babylon's golden cup —"full of abominations and filthiness of her fornications" (Rev. 17:4). What Erikson calls "female inner space" is disgusting, dirty, and contaminating. For Swift, the anal orifice is a metaphor for all female apertures; excrement is then the final distillation of Caelia's other remains—her dirt, sweat, dandruff, hair,

scabs, slops, ear wax, teeth scrapings, snot, grease, etc. Her chamber pot may
have ornaments to disguise its function, but the male is not fooled for a minute.
Surely Strephon cannot be criticized for not wanting to search for hope at the
bottom of this Pandora's box. Like Gulliver, Rasselas (1759), the speaker of *An
Essay on Man* (1733–34), and Matthew Bramble in *Humphrey Clinker* (1771),
Strephon discovers the vanity of human wishes in his "grand survey." He is, however, punished for peeping; his imagination is tainted (by the Goddess of Ven-
geance), so that all the women he sees are associated with Caelia's box.

Caelia's notions, potions, and lotions cannot be considered a synecdoche for
Western civilization. Nor is there textual evidence that Strephon is punished because he worshiped Caelia as a paragon. Admittedly, at the end of *The Lady's
Dressing Room*, the speaker does seem to castigate Strephon for rejecting all
women:

> I pity wretched *Strephon* blind
> To all the Charms of Female Kind;
> Should I the Queen of Love refuse,
> Because she rose from stinking Ooze?
> To him that looks behind the Scene,
> *Satira's* but some pocky Queen.
> When *Celia* in her Glory shows,
> If *Strephon* would but stop his Nose;
> (Who now so impiously blasphemes
> Her Ointments, Daubs, and Paints and Creams,
> Her Washes, Slops, and every Clout,
> With which he makes so foul a Rout;)
> He soon would learn to think like me,
> And bless his ravisht Sight to see
> Such Order from Confusion sprung,
> Such gaudy Tulips rais'd from Dung.
>
> (129–44)

By presumably accepting the Queen of Love, the poet seems to differentiate himself from Strephon, who has been condemned to reject women. At the same
time, however, Strephon is blind to a glory in the female sex that the speaker can
only appreciate by holding his nose. Having perceived the confusion behind the
order, the dung beneath the tulips, Strephon recognizes the diseased actress behind the stage presence. Strephon is in fact condemned to reality; his blindness is
an insight, while the alternative to blindness is the poet's "ravisht Sight," surely
an ambivalent term. Does the Queen of Love transport or violate her votaries?
Does the speaker's perception, his acceptance of the female facade, represent an
elevated or raped consciousness? Is not "ravisht Sight" also a kind of blindness?

Surely this speaker is closer to Strephon than he admits. Has not his own song, *The Lady's Dressing Room*, "impiously blasphemed" against ointments and paints, washes and slops? Perhaps the queen (who is after all a Queen of Ooze) *should* be refused, since even her carefully crafted appearance is gaudy and smelly.

In many of his "obscene" poems, Swift examined the role deception plays in the creation of a saving but inadequate fiction of femininity. He wrote poems about prudes who bare their heaving bosoms in church under the guise of religiosity and run away with the butler only to become his clap-ridden whore, about May-December marriages in which the poor old dean is cuckolded and his widow poxed, poems about female-induced impotence and imprudence, about card games and shopping and gossiping—all forms of pretense. Furniture, not ideas, inhabits the minds of these women: their hearts are as hard and senseless as an ivory table book. Women who seem spiritual, beautiful, and healthy are shown to be physical, ugly, and diseased. Modesty is only vanity, and the semblance of order hides decay. Female sexuality is equated with degeneration, disease, and death. In *A Beautiful Young Nymph* (1731), Swift describes the undressing of a battered prostitute, as she removes her hair, her crystal eye, her teeth, her stuffing—disrobing is a kind of dismemberment. The morning after requires the decrepit whore to employ all her "arts" to reconstruct her "scatter'd Parts" (67–68). In contrast to Herrick's Corinna, that "sweet slugabed" who is entreated to come forth "like the spring time, fresh and green" (Corinna's Going A-maying" [1648], 16), Swift's "Corinna in the Morning dizen'd, / Who sees, will spew; who smells, be poison'd" (73–74). Destroyed by syphilis, Corinna is corroding matter personified. Similarly, the waking Diana of *The Progress of Beauty* (1719–20) is a mingled mass of dirt and sweat with cracked lips, foul teeth, and gummy eyes. With the painter's arts, she manages to reconstruct herself in four hours, adoring the effect of her own craft. Like the moon and the Queen of Love, Diana can "Delude at once and Bless our Sight" (70) chiefly by appearing after the sun goes down. She too is waning, bit by bit rotting away; for eventually, with no matter left, all forms fail:

> But, Art no longer can prevayl
> When the Materialls all are gone,
> The best Mechanick Hand must Fayl
> Where Nothing's left to work upon.
>
> Matter, as wise Logicians say,
> Cannot without a Form subsist,
> And Form, say I, as well as They,
> Must fayl if Matter bring no Grist.
>   (77–84)

Even more blunt is Swift's reminder that "No Painting can restore a Nose" (111).

Male critics who have seen these poems as affirmations of life and body are ignoring the impact of the gross and filthy on characters and readers alike: "Fine ideas vanish fast, / While all the gross and filthy last" (*Strephon and Chloe*, 333–34). Regardless of how silly the Strephons are, they do not frighten us with their physicality; Chloe, Caelia, Corinna, and Diana, on the other hand, remind us too vividly of the gruesome implications of temporal and biological existence. Artists manqué, these women can only temporarily stave off the inevitable end. The arts of paint, patches, and billet-doux, the dressing-room rites of pride, the stratagems of the politician, the puppeteer, the stage actress—these cannot transfigure or even successfully hide the dreaded signs of mortality.

It is no wonder, then, that the Augustan satirist attacked the female scribbler so virulently. Female writers are maligned as failures because they cannot transcend their bodily limitations; they cannot conceive of themselves in any but reproductive terms. A prototype of the female dunce, Phoebe Clinket of *Three Hours after Marriage* (1717) lovingly nurtures the unworthy issue of her muse as proof of the "Fertility and Readiness" of her imagination: she is, ironically, as sensual and indiscriminate in her poetic strainings as Lady Townley in her insatiable erotic longings. Female writers are likened to mothers of illegitimate or misshapen offspring: they are not producing what they ought to; their labors result only in stillborn objects or abortions. It makes perfect sense, then, that a loose lady novelist should be the first prize in the urinary contest of *The Dunciad* (1728, 1743), while a chamber pot is held out for the runner-up. But the other side of the satirist's anger, indeed the reason for it, is an implied recognition of himself in her. Both the female coquette and the female dunce represent the satirist's nervousness about his own use of form to control corruption; they represent a dark parody of the satirist himself.

The debased arts of the female serve the Scriblerians as an emblem of the corruption of literary and ethical standards in Walpole's England. Pope, Arbuthnot, Gay, and Fielding frequently portray their disgust with middle-class materialism in the female's capitulation to her body; their horror of a society dedicated to acquisitive enterprise is pictured in female pride; their anger at the end of classical and Christian humanism and the imminent death of culture, characterized by effeminate, corrupt genres and a sentimental audience lacking both taste and learning, is revealed in female mindlessness and the lazy delusions of love she engenders. In this respect, the Scriblerians continue the tradition of Revelation, which treats the harlot as a symbol of the abominations of the great city.

But the coquette/whore in Augustan satire is not the only female whose arts become a metaphor for the failure of art to redeem the time. As if to substantiate Karen Horney's view that figures like the sphinx, Circe, and Kali reveal how male dread of women masks resentment of the female's ability to be passively sexual, as if to substantiate the belief that male fear of women is related to womb envy, Swift and Pope reserve their most impassioned attacks on female creativity for monstrous mothers who come to represent the sterility of indiscriminate fecundity, encroaching entropy, and the failure of form.

In one of his earliest prose pieces, *The Battle of the Books* (1704), Swift describes the struggle between Modern hacks and the Ancient poets who have created the traditions of Western civilization, The Moderns worship the Goddess Criticism, the personification of pedantry and miseducation, who devours numberless volumes in her den, surrounded by her relatives and children—Ignorance, Pride, Opinion, Noise, Impudence, Dullness, Vanity, Positiveness, Pedantry, and Ill-Manners:

> The Goddess herself had Claws like a Cat: Her Head, and Ears, and Voice, resembled those of an Ass; Her Teeth fallen out before; Her Eyes turned inward, as if she lookt only upon herself; Her Diet was the overflowing of her own *Gall*: Her *Spleen* was so large, as to stand prominent like a Dug of the first Rate, nor wanted Excrescencies in form of Teats, at which a Crew of ugly Monsters were greedily sucking; and, what is wonderful to conceive, the bulk of Spleen increased faster than the Sucking could diminish it.

As a nursing mother who sustains and even embodies the inky productivity of second-rate artists, philosophers, and scholars, Criticism directly recalls Spenser's portrait of Errour at the beginning of *The Faerie Queene*. Half serpent, half woman, monstrous Errour also inhabits a den where she nurses uncouth shapes at her poisonous dugs (1.1.14–22). And just as Criticism turns herself into an octavo, Errour's vomit consists of books and papers as well as frogs and toads. Errour's classical prototypes, the monstrous Echidna and Chimaera, were both associated with rhetorical persuasion and fake erudition in the Renaissance.

Because criticism is also heretical, Swift uses his goddess to evoke simultaneously the repellent figure of Sin in *Paradise Lost* ([1667] 2.865–70). Milton's version of the classical Gorgon suckles insatiable grotesques while barking hell hounds creep in and out of her womb. Half woman, half serpent, Milton's monstrous Sin is a grotesque parody of the son of God, since this daughter pictures herself at the right hand of *her* divine father, Satan. A negative emblem of motherhood, Sin is also a dark forewarning of the only other female in *Paradise Lost*— the first human mother, Eve, who also heeds the advice of the snake and thereby brings sin and suffering into what was paradise. Making explicit what Spenser and Swift merely intimate, Milton calls Sin's first child "Death." The eternal breeding, eating, spewing, feeding, and redevouring that characterize Errour, Sin, and Criticism link them to biological cycles considered destructive to intellectual and spiritual forms of life. All three mothers threaten to overwhelm the poets with their ceaseless production of deformities who will overrun civilization. Since all the creations of the mother are excretions, since all the excretions of the mother are her food and her weapon, each mother forms with her brood a self-enclosed system—cannibalistic and solipsistic. The creativity of the word made flesh is annihilating.

The goddess from whose dugs spleen issues cannot be far removed from the Goddess of Spleen in *The Rape of the Lock*. The parent of the vapours and female wit, the hysteric or poetic fit, the Queen of Spleen rules over all women between the ages of fifteen and fifty. Because she is associated with the same anticreation of formlessness that characterizes Errour, Sin, and Criticism, she illuminates Pope's later interest in Mary Toft, who reputedly gave birth to seventeen rabbits. The doctor who discovered and then exposed the case as a fraud appears in *The Dunciad* delivering the gold in Annius's feces. Birth has become a grotesque testimonial to the filthy materiality of life. Biological creation is presented as the dirty and egotistical acquisition of filthy lucre accomplished by contaminated men, feminized men, who embrace the way of matter too soft, the way of excrement, the woman's way of death.

Drawing on the genealogy of dark, dull goddesses who generate and nurture death, Pope's Goddess of Dullness is a fitting culmination to the line that traces back to Swift's Criticism, Milton's Sin, and Spenser's Errour. The monstrous woman symbolizes the failure of culture, the failure of art, and the death of the satirist. Worshiped by a society of dunces, the Mighty Mother of Dullness rules her brood of pedantic critics, flattering hacks, and self-serving educators by female wiles. In book 1 of *The Dunciad in Four Books* (1743), she wishfully envisions her domain:

> O! When shall rise a Monarch all our own,
> And I, a Nursing-mother, rock the throne,
> 'Twixt Prince and People close the Curtain draw,
> Shade him from Light, and cover him from Law;
> Fatten the Courtier, starve the learned band,
> And suckle Armies, and dry-nurse the land:
> 'Till Senates nod to Lullabies divine,
> And all be sleep, as at an Ode of thine!
>
> (1.331–18)

Indeed in book 4 ([1742] 1743) the enormous daughter of chaos and night rocks the laureate in her ample lap while handing out rewards and intoxicating drinks to her dull sons. Prince and people are effectively divorced by a government that bribes when not fiddling, dancing, or playing cricket. The imbibing and eating increase her family's weight, contributing to the general inertia and laziness. She is one more avatar of the Queen of Ooze, of the Queen of Spleen, of that entire sex of queens. She nods, and all of nature falls asleep. In the milk of her kindness, her unthinking and self-aggrandizing blanket affection, this Queen of Love encourages a security that breeds mediocrity and passivity and spreads her contagious meaninglessness throughout the land.

Behind his enlightened humanism, the gloom of the Tory satirist extends to the implied concession that his own art is quite probably inadequate. The satirist who has refused to please by any but manly ways finds it impossible to purge a society gone effeminate. The dreaded female has triumphed. Be she glittering coquette, bovine mother, or diseased whore, she symbolizes the sundry humiliations of dehumanization. The female is despised and feared because she obliterates all distinctions, forecasts the onrushing apocalypse. Thus she illustrates Simone de Beauvoir's thesis that the female has been made to represent man's ambivalent feelings about his inability to control his own existence, his own birth and death. As the Other, the woman is associated with contingency, with life made to be destroyed: "It is the horror of his own carnal contingence, which he projects upon her." By projecting it as a detested attribute which defines the monstrous female, the satirist can escape recognition of his own immanence. However, since the monstrous female emerges finally as the very source and justification of his art, the satirist assures his own complicity: not only does he derive his meaning from her, he also creates the reasons for his own inescapable submission to her. As much as the satirist despises Nature, he cherishes the biological life that is necessary for his very existence. Similarly, his passionate commitment to portraying the female monster repeatedly in all her power and energy implies that he sees her as not only his negation but also his raison d'être. If the monstrous woman allows the satirist to exorcise his fear of mortality and physicality by projecting it onto the Other, she can also function as a sign of his fascination with materiality, his need to identify himself with his body, his temptation to succumb to his culture and thereby end his lonely protest. She is, in other words, a fascinating alternative, a way of leaving the burdens of self and excellence behind. The satirist can control his ambivalent response to his culture and his body by attacking both in the eternal Other, the female whose song he hymns with such fury. Indeed the hostility and aggression in satire may well survive topicality, because its fictions describe our most secret and shameful fantasies of munching on baby shanks, sinking into the oblivion of sleep, or identifying ourselves with our bodies. Used to objectify his own rejected desires and doubts, the female is a sign of the satirist's self-division. The failure of love, then, is not simply a subject of Augustan satire. It is perhaps its implied origin.

Even more important, the use of the woman to represent these anxiously ambiguous attitudes can help explain why H.D. and Muriel Rukeyser wrote as the sphinx, why Emily Dickinson and Sylvia Plath portray themselves as witches while Maxine Kumin speaks as a Medusa. Throughout male literary history, gorgons, sirens, mothers of death, and goddesses of night represent women who reject passivity and silence. Thus in the nineteenth century the romantics are haunted by characters like Geraldine and Lamia—two snaky sorceresses closely associated with the powerful, sensual illusions of art. In the realistic novel, moreover, an imaginative girl like Becky Sharp quickly degenerates into a vicious temptress whose tail, thrashing in the lower depths, is barely glimpsed by her creator, Thackeray. Each portrait of the female monster is a forceful persuasion against female creativity that has surely inhibited many women from attempting the pen, even as it suggested to those who managed to write that they were somehow unnatural and dangerous in their craft. But besides contributing to a specifically female anxiety of authorship, the female monster surely sustains the alienation so many women feel from our bodies, our selves. The pruning and preening, the mirror madness, the concern with odors and aging, with hair too curly or too lank, with bodies too thin or thick: all these motifs in women's lives and literature imply our dread of being identified as female monsters. Perhaps it is for this reason that, in a poem entitled *Hypocrite Woman*, Denise Levertov considers the woman's hatred of her own body something "drifting through western air," a lesson taught by "a white sweating bull of a poet." Surely she is right to connect such self-loathing with the paring of our dreams which, for too long now, we have "clipped . . . like ends of / split hair."

ELLEN POLLAK

Comment on Susan Gubar's
"The Female Monster
in Augustan Satire"

Although it is in many ways a fascinating discussion of women in Augustan satire, Susan Gubar's treatment of the image of the female monster in the works of the Scriblerians seems to me marred by the author's tendency to work backward from an externally defined archetype to specific literary texts. Starting with the premise that male-created literary images of female grotesques constitute projections of male anxiety and ambivalence about female sexuality and control, Gubar explicates a series of texts which make recurrent use of images of female monsters as if the texts themselves were just such projections—as if, in effect, the works of Swift and his contemporaries equaled the images they exploit.

Now early eighteenth-century English literature does reflect an unusual, even anxious, preoccupation with women and their place in society, and this preoccupation does commonly express itself in concepts of female deviancy. Indeed, an analysis of the literature of the age—from popular fiction to feminine conduct manuals and periodical literature—reveals the existence by the 1680's of a pervasive social mythology of passive womanhood that upheld a rigorously defined ideal of woman as married, conjugally faithful, modest, good-natured, cheerfully tolerant of idleness, and preeminently intent on pleasing her husband, while it placed a negative value on all women who strayed from these often impossible and contradictory expectations, generating as its most popular stock deviants the figures of coquette, prude, pedant, and superannuated virgin or old maid. But as Elizabeth Janeway has shown, it is of paramount importance for analysts of culture to distinguish between the realms of myth, art, and neurosis. While the

From *Signs: Journal of Women in Culture and Society* 3, no. 3 (Spring 1978). © 1978 by The University of Chicago.

distortions of neurosis are private, those of myth have public meaning and are bound up with social and economic realities. Art, in turn, uses but is not the same as myth. When Gubar treats Swift's literary use of female grotesques and the crazed projections of the Gulliver he created as equivalent examples of male "inability to accept . . . the human condition," these categories become dangerously confused.

A more historical approach to the same body of works, in fact, reveals that the pervasiveness of themes of female promiscuity had roots in certain important social and economic developments that took place in the seventeenth century. A change in property law, such as the strict settlement, for example, helped to shift the burden of civil responsibility for conjugal infidelity almost exclusively onto women. Designed to prevent heirs from breaking up estates, this legal device enabled landowners not only to project plans for their estates onto future generations but also to entail all their property in each generation on a single heir, thus exacerbating the damaging effects of bastardy on the lineal descent of family wealth. In an economy where commercial prosperity and increased social mobility were posing an uncommon threat to an already diluted aristocracy, and where women—who played a crucial if indirect role in the enlargement of estates—were experiencing an unprecedented degree of leisure, social anxiety over the chastity of wives was, not surprisingly, intensified.

Attention to the social and economic realities being mediated by the popular myths of the age is essential to an appreciation of what were really striking differences among the Scriblerians in their treatment of women—differences which Gubar's archetypal approach inevitably obscures. As Charles Kerby-Miller makes clear in the preface to his edition of the Scriblerus satires, the group was not a "typical gathering of like-minded men," but rather "a merger of two literary groups, one led by Swift and the other by Pope . . . and the motives of their leaders were by no means similar." In fact, it is likely that one of Swift's hopes in joining the scheme was to win Pope and Gay away from the influence of Addison and Steele, whom the Dean repudiated not only for their Whig principles but for an exploitative and patronizing attitude toward the "fair sex," evidenced in their urbane tolerance of women's "little Vanities and Follies" as negative yet somehow irresistibly appealing. Comic deflation of the threat of female deviancy is common in the works of Pope and Gay, as it is in those of Addison and Steele, and, in my opinion, has precisely the *opposite* effect of the female grotesques that appear in the poems of Jonathan Swift.

Twenty years Swift's junior, Pope was much more comfortably identified than the Dean with the bourgeois culture that generated the myth of passive womanhood and its stereotypic negative exempla. When he wrote the *Rape of the Lock*, he exploited this mythology for all its paradoxes and poetic possibilities, pitting the twin freaks of coquette and prude against one another in perfect dialectical symmetry. Belinda may be the Circe at the center of this poem, but she is tamed. As a "Vessel" (2.47) carrying all the "glitt'ring Spoil" (1.132) of the world, she herself is identified with that world and, like nature, is to be conquered, ransacked, and possessed by commercial man. As compulsive consumer, she is not only the bearer of but a testimony to British national wealth. Her narcissism, though satirized according to propriety as unfeminine and subversive, is also glorified as keeping commerce in motion. In short, as coquette and lady of quality, Belinda occupies as necessary a place in the providential order assumed by mercantile rationalism as ever Martha Blount did in her role as domestic ideal. In Pope's vision, the self-centered tease is ultimately justified and, in the process, robbed of her independent force by being brought into line with male economic needs. Her display of her beauty is identified with his display of his booty, her enslavement of and ultimate triumph over man through her powers of attraction with his blissful "living Death" (5.61, 78).

As Gubar notes, Swift's poems never achieve the degree of integration evidenced in Pope's. But instead of attributing their dissonance to the Dean's more virulent contempt for women, I see it as a reflection of his failure ever to come to terms with the conventions "modern" culture made available to him for writing about the female sex. With one foot in the Restoration and the other in the eighteenth century, he could tear away at the sentimentalizations of women that became fashionable in the reign of Queen Anne, but he lacked an appropriately comprehensive language or epistemology for embodying an alternative ideal in any but negative satiric terms. Such negatively conceived satire was a mode of liberation for Swift. Lacking faith in the commonplaces of ancient literary tradition, but despising the available modern alternatives, he established a rhetorical art through which he could free himself from the limits of both. By donning the literary vestures of the virtuoso modern writer and appropriating them for his own satiric uses through irony, he managed, in *A Tale of a Tub*, to mourn the passing of a culture in the very act of becoming a modern writer. And in Gulliver he exposed the insanity of naive, utopian rationalism in its comic as well as tragic dimensions; for Gulliver's disgust with his fellow mortals at the end of his travels is clearly more a mad than a model solution to the problem of being human. Similarly, if Swift creates mad or obsessive visions of women in his verse, he does so quite self-consciously and, finally, only to expose the inadequacy of such perspectives. Indeed, I would agree with Gubar that it is precisely because Swift was aware of the impact of "the gross and filthy"—of their power to embarrass a world concerned to keep appearances—that he exploits them so archly in his verse; but he does so in a way that ultimately challenges his readers to reevaluate their responses to the excremental facts of life. If you're shocked by the fact that Caelia shits, *Cassinus and Peter* warns, you're a fool too! And it is precisely *because* the solution proffered at the end of *Strephon and Chloe* seems inadequate to the realities which the characters confront that we are invited to readjust our notions of what is possible. The last lines of this poem turn on the pivotal or "key" word "Decency." In line 252, the word "decent" clearly is used ironically to satirize the superficial, vulgar, and hypocritical values of a society that prescribes deception as the proper way for women to sustain an illusion of divinity. But in the final stanza, "Decency" takes on a more inclusive meaning, suggesting a notion of mutual human tolerance as a stable adhesive of life-long love, esteem, and friendship. This mode of shifting perspective through the multiple possibilities of a single word is typical in Swift, occurring in *A Beautiful Young Nymph Going to Bed* with a play on the word "bashful" (l. 71) and in a number of interesting ways in "Corinna."

In *Cadenus and Vanessa*, the appeal to divine powers for the creation of miraculous Vanessa was a function of Swift's need to extricate Esther Vanhomrigh from the stifling categories and "common forms" (l. 612) of a world in which a woman of her ilk was, by definition, an eccentric. Vanessa's origins at the hands of Venus and Pallas mark her as a thoroughly "unconventional" female human being embodying both erotic and intellectual dimensions—a creature for whom the English language offered no positive or adequate term. Swift could name her only by negation as "A Nymph so hard to be subdu'd / Who neither was Coquette nor Prude" (ll. 496–97). Both Venus and Cadenus in a sense create a monster in Vanessa; but though scheming, projecting Venus is self-defeated in her attempt to restore her reign, it is not at all clear that Cadenus, despite age and initial embarrassment, is not equal to the alternative possibility that Vanessa represents (ll. 818–27). As an aging scholar he is, after all, as ill suited for love in society's eyes as she is for learning. Surely the complex process by which Swift imagines Hessy as a positive synthesis of the qualities his society took for granted as mutually exclusive in women is very different—indeed, precisely the reverse—of that by which Pope idealizes single, childless Martha Blount at the end of *To a Lady* by transforming her into the perfect wife and mother!

So, if Swift's women often overwhelm and repel, it is at least in part because he lacked what Pope possessed—the security of faith in a myth of idleness and domestication on the basis of which he could shape his literary representations of them. This hardly disassociates the Dean from the patriarchalism that has pervaded Western culture for centuries and is still deeply embedded in our language and traditions, but it does disassociate him in important ways from an essentially middle-class sexual ideology that crystallized during his lifetime and from which he expressed explicit alienation. Feminist criticism has as much to learn from the ways in which men could or could not and did or did not come to terms with the sexual norms of their societies as it does from the devastating problems such norms have created for women. It would be a shame if feminist inquiry closed doors to an understanding of the rhetorical and emotional struggles confronted by either men or women engaged in literary activity within the context of cultural and linguistic institutions which have often tyrannically defined the limits of expression. In its stance of resistance to what Ian Watt has called the "decarnalisation of the public feminine role," Swift's work can provide us with an unusual and instructive, prenovelistic perspective on a body of attitudes that unfortunately happen to be part of our heritage.

SUSAN GUBAR

Reply to Pollak

As I pointed out, critics of Greene's persuasion have traditionally insisted on justifying Swift's portraits of filthy females by claiming his ironic attack is leveled against male mystifications of women. But, in the process of deflating the romantic stereotype of angelic purity, Swift implies that for women to be human means to be monstrous. While I remain unconvinced that Swift praises the fuming goddess Cloacine for purely pedagogic purposes, I am indebted to Pollak for pointing out the quite divergent uses to which the female monster could be put by Swift and Pope. Actually, though, I would argue further that the differences between their personal and social attitudes toward women are quite small in scale compared with the wide-ranging positions distinguishing writers like Spenser, Milton, Coleridge, Keats, and Thackeray, all of whom are also obsessed with the female monster. What this implies, then, is that, regardless of the lesson she purportedly teaches, the female monster is a crucial symbol for radically different writers, all of whom exploit her fall into immanence to make it symbolize any number of contradictory attitudes, each of which would of course benefit from historical study of its legal, social, and political implications.

While it is true that I have tried to define a neurotic strain that runs throughout western European literary culture, I fail to see why this approach is necessarily "archetypal" since I am hardly arguing that the female monster is an eternal verity. Instead, I would only claim that her persistent presence points to the deep misogyny of what Gertrude Stein called "Patriarchal Poetry." Furthermore, my

essay begins with the poetry of Adrienne Rich and closes with that of Denise
Levertov because I am concerned with the effects of such images on women,
specifically on women writers (since the female monster is patriarchy's version of
the creative woman). While Pollak examines satire as "a mode of liberation for
Swift," I study it as a mode of imprisonment for the woman reader who experiences herself as trapped within the satirist's text. Like Christina Rossetti's model
"In an Artist's Studio," such a woman is haunted by alien visions of herself —
"not as she is, but as she fills his dreams."

Chronology

1667	Jonathan Swift born in Dublin to English parents; father dies.
1674–82	Studies at Kilkenny School.
1682–88	Trinity College, Dublin; B.A. *speciali gratia* 1684; work toward M.A. interrupted by Glorious Revolution.
1689–94	Secretary to Sir William Temple, Moor Park; meets Stella; first outbreak of Ménière's disease probably in 1690.
1694	Takes Anglican deacon's orders.
1695	Ordained priest in the Church of Ireland; moves to Kilroot parish, where he probably writes *A Tale of a Tub* (1697–98?).
1699–1710	Appointments and livings in the Church of Ireland. As domestic chaplain to the Earl of Berkeley, Lord Justice of Ireland, Swift begins his career of defender of the rights of the Church of Ireland, working with the Whigs.
1704	*A Tale of a Tub* and *The Battle of the Books* published.
1707	Meets Vanessa.
1708–09	*The Bickerstaff Papers.*
1709	With Steele, founds the *Tatler.*
1710	Goes over to the Tories.
1713	Appointed Dean of St. Patrick's Cathedral, Dublin; from this time lives mostly in Ireland.
1724–25	*Drapier's Letters.*

157

1726   *Gulliver's Travels* published.

1729   *A Modest Proposal.*

1742   Declared insane.

1745   Dies; buried in St. Patrick's Cathedral.

Contributors

HAROLD BLOOM, Sterling Professor of the Humanities at Yale University, is the author of *The Anxiety of Influence*, *Poetry and Repression*, and many other volumes of literary criticism. His forthcoming study, *Freud: Transference and Authority*, attempts a full-scale reading of all Freud's major writings. A MacArthur Prize Fellow, he is general editor of five series of literary criticism published by Chelsea House.

KATHLEEN WILLIAMS is Professor of English at the University of California at Riverside; she has written extensively on Swift.

ROBERT C. ELLIOTT taught at the University of California at San Diego. His books include *The Literary Persona*, *The Poetry of Jonathan Swift*, *The Power of Satire: Magic, Ritual, Art*, and *The Shape of Utopia: Studies in a Literary Genre*.

RONALD PAULSON is Professor of English at The Johns Hopkins University. Among his works are *The Fictions of Satire*, *Satire and the Novel in Eighteenth-Century England*, *Theme and Structure in Swift's* Tale of a Tub, *The Art of Hogarth*, *Emblem and Expression: Meaning in English Art of the Eighteenth Century*, and *Literary Landscape: Turner and Constable*.

MARTIN PRICE is Sterling Professor of English Literature at Yale University and the author of *Swift's Rhetorical Art: A Study in Structure and Meaning*, *To the Palace of Wisdom: Studies in Order and Energy From Dryden to Blake*, *Forms of Life: Character and Moral Imagination in the Novel*, and other works.

PAUL FUSSELL teaches in the Department of English at the University of Pennsylvania. Some of his books are *Abroad: British Literary Traveling Between the Wars*, *The Great War and Modern Memory*, *Poetic Meter and Poetic Form*, *Theory of Prosody in Eighteenth-Century England*, *The Rhetorical World of Augustan Humanism: Ethics and Imagery from Swift to Burke*, and *Samuel Johnson and the Life of Writing*.

CLAUDE RAWSON is Senior Lecturer at the University of Warwick. His works on Swift include *Gulliver and the Gentle Reader: Studies in Swift and Our Time*, and the anthologies *Focus: Swift* and *The Character of Swift's Satire: A Revised Focus*.

PATRICIA MEYER SPACKS is Professor of English at Yale University and author of *The Insistence of Horror: Aspects of the Supernatural in 18th-Century Poetry*, *The Adolescent Idea: Myths of Youth and the Adult Imagination*, *The Female Imagination*, and other works. Most recently she has published *Gossip*.

PETER STEELE, S. J., is Tutor in English at the University of Melbourne. He has written articles on literature and theology and *Jonathan Swift: Preacher and Jester*.

DAVID NOKES teaches at King's College, London.

SUSAN GUBAR teaches in the Department of English at Indiana University. Together with Sandra M. Gilbert she has written *The Madwoman in the Attic: A Study of Women and the Literary Imagination in the Nineteenth Century* and edited *Shakespeare's Sisters: Feminist Essays on Women Poets*.

ELLEN POLLAK teaches in the Department of English at the University of Pennsylvania.

Bibliography

Battestin, Martin C. *The Providence of Wit: Aspects of Form in Augustan Literature and the Arts.* Oxford: Oxford University Press, 1974.

Bentman, Raymond. "Satiric Structure and Tone in the Conclusion of *Gulliver's Travels.*" *Studies in English Literature 1500–1900* 11 (1971): 535–48.

Bogel, Fredric V. "Irony, Inference, and Critical Uncertainty." *Yale Review* 69, no. 4 (1980): 503–19.

Brown, Norman O. *Life Against Death: The Psychoanalytical Meaning of History.* Middletown, Conn.: Wesleyan University Press, 1959.

Champion, Larry S. "Gulliver's Voyages: The Framing Events as a Guide to Interpretation." *Texas Studies in Literature and Language* 10 (1969): 529–36.

————, ed. *Quick Springs of Sense.* Athens, Ga.: University of Georgia Press, 1974.

Clark, John R. *Form and Frenzy in Swift's* Tale of a Tub. Ithaca: Cornell University Press, 1970.

————. "Initiation Rite: Swift's *Modest Proposal,* Sentence 1." *American Notes and Queries* 14 (1975): 20–21.

Clifford, Gay. *The Transformations of Allegory.* London: Routledge and Kegan Paul, 1974.

Ewald, William B. *The Masks of Jonathan Swift.* Cambridge: Harvard University Press, 1954.

Fabricant, Carole. *Swift's Landscape.* Baltimore: The Johns Hopkins University Press, 1982.

Fischer, John, and Donald Mell, eds. *Contemporary Studies of Swift's Poetry.* Newark, Del.: University of Delaware Press,

Fussell, Paul. *Rhetorical World of Augustan Humanism.* Oxford: Oxford University Press, 1965.

Harth, Phillip. *Swift and Anglican Rationalism: The Religious Background of* A Tale of a Tub. Chicago: The University of Chicago Press, 1961.

Hilson, J.C., et al., eds. *Augustan Worlds: New Essays on Eighteenth-Century Literature.* Leicester: Leicester University Press, 1978.

Huxley, Aldous. "Swift." In *Do What You Will.* London: Chatto and Windus, 1929.

Jeffares, A. Norman, ed. *Swift: Modern Judgements.* London: Macmillan, 1969.

Johnson, Maurice. *The Sin of Wit: Jonathan Swift as a Poet.* Syracuse, N.Y.: Syracuse University Press, 1950.

Korkowski, Eugene. "Swift's Tub: Traditional Emblem and Proverbial Enigma." *Eighteenth-Century Life* 4 (1978): 100–103.

Leavis, F.R. "The Irony of Swift." In *Determinations*. London: Chatto and Windus, 1934.

Lockwood, Thomas. "The Augustan Author-Audience Relationship: Satiric vs. Comic Forms." *ELH* 36 (1969): 648–58.

————. "Swift's *Modest Proposal*: An Interpretation." *Papers on Language and Literature* 10, no. 3 (1975): 254–67.

Mack, Maynard, and I. Gregor, eds. *Imagined Worlds: Essays on Some English Novels and Novelists in Honour of John Butt*. London: Methuen, 1968.

Murry, John Middleton. *Jonathan Swift: A Critical Biography*. New York: Noonday Press, 1955.

Orwell, George. "Politics vs. Literature: An Examination of *Gulliver's Travels*." In *The Collected Essays, Journalism and Letters of George Orwell*. London: Secker and Warburg, 1968.

Paulson, Ronald. *The Fictions of Satire*. Baltimore: The Johns Hopkins Press, 1967.

————, ed. *Satire: Modern Essays in Criticism*. Englewood Cliffs, N.J.: Prentice-Hall, 1971.

————. *Theme and Structure in Swift's* Tale of a Tub. New Haven: Yale University Press, 1960.

Probyn, Clive, ed. *The Art of Jonathan Swift*. New York: Barnes and Noble; London: Vision Press, 1978.

Quilligan, Maureen. *The Language of Allegory*. Ithaca: Cornell University Press, 1979.

Quinlan, Maurice. "Swift's Use of Literalization as a Rhetorical Device." *Publications of the MLA of America* 82 (1967): 516–21.

Quintana, Ricardo. *The Mind and Art of Jonathan Swift*. New York and London: Oxford University Press, 1936.

Rawson, Claude J., ed. *The Character of Swift's Satire: A Revised Focus*. Newark, Del.: University of Delaware Press, 1983.

————, ed. *Focus: Swift*. London: Sphere Books, 1971.

Reed, Gail S. "Dr. Greenacre and Captain Gulliver: Notes on Conventions of Interpretation and Reading." *Literature and Psychology* 26 (1976): 185–90.

Rees, Christine. "Gay, Swift, and the Nymphs of Drury-Lane." *Essays in Criticism* 26, no. 3 (1976): 219–35.

Rodino, Richard H. "Varieties of Vexatious Experience in Swift and Others." *Papers on Language and Literature* 18, no. 3 (1982): 325–47.

Rogers, Pat. *The Augustan Vision*. New York: Barnes and Noble, 1974.

————. *Grub Street: Studies in a Subculture*. London: Methuen, 1972.

Said, Edward. *Beginnings: Intention and Method*. New York: Basic Books, 1975.

Smith, Frederik. *Language and Reality in Swift's* A Tale of a Tub. Columbus: Ohio State University Press, 1979.

Steele, Peter. *Jonathan Swift: Preacher and Jester*. Oxford: Oxford University Press, 1978.

Tuveson, Ernest. *Swift: A Collection of Critical Essays*. Englewood Cliffs, N.J.: Prentice-Hall, 1964.

Vickers, Brian, ed. *The World of Jonathan Swift: Essays for the Tercentenary*. Cambridge: Harvard University Press; Oxford: Basil Blackwell, 1968.

Williams, Kathleen. *Jonathan Swift and the Age of Compromise*. Lawrence: University of Kansas Press, 1958.

Woolf, Virginia. "Swift's *Journal to Stella*." In *The Second Common Reader*. London: Hogarth Press, 1932.

Acknowledgments

"Giddy Circumstance" by Kathleen Williams from *Jonathan Swift and the Age of Compromise* by Kathleen Williams, © 1958 by the University of Kansas Press. Reprinted by permission.

"The Satirist Satirized" by Robert C. Elliott from *The Power of Satire: Magic, Ritual, Art* by Robert C. Elliott, © 1960 by Princeton University Press. Reprinted by permission of Princeton University Press.

"The Parody of Eccentricity" by Ronald Paulson from *Theme and Structure in Swift's "Tale of a Tub,"* by Ronald Paulson, © 1960 by Yale University Press. Reprinted by permission.

"Swift: Order and Obligation" by Martin Price from *To the Palace of Wisdom* by Martin Price, ©1964 by Martin Price. Reprinted by permission of Southern Illinois University Press and Feffer & Simons, Inc.

"The Paradox of Man" by Paul Fussell from *The Rhetorical World of Augustan Humanism* by Paul Fussell, © 1965 by Oxford University Press. Reprinted by permission.

"Order and Cruelty: A Reading of Swift (with some comments on Pope and Johnson)" by Claude Rawson from *Essays in Criticism* 20, no. 1 (January 1977), © 1970 by *Essays in Criticism*. Reprinted by permission.

"Some Reflections on Satire" by Patricia Meyer Spacks from *Genre* 1, no. 1 (January 1968), © 1967 by the Editors of *Genre*. (Australia) This essay later appeared in *Satire: Modern Essays in Criticism* (Prentice-Hall, 1971). Reprinted by permission.

"Terminal Days among the Houyhnhnms" by Peter Steele from *Southern Review* 4, no. 3 (1971), © 1971 by the University of Adelaide. Reprinted by permission.

"Swift and the Beggars" by David Nokes from *Essays in Criticism* 26, no. 3 (July 1976), © 1976 by *Essays in Criticism*. Reprinted by permission.

"The Female Monster in Augustan Satire" by Susan Gubar from *Signs: Journal of Women in Culture and Society* 3, no. 2 (Winter 1977), © 1977 by The University of Chicago. Reprinted by permission of The University of Chicago Press.

"Comment on Susan Gubar's 'The Female Monster in Augustan Satire' " by Ellen Pollak from *Signs: Journal of Women in Culture and Society* 3, no. 3 (Spring 1978), © 1978 by The University of Chicago. Reprinted by permission of The University of Chicago Press.

Index